The ABC of Socialism

John Rees

COUNTERFIRE publication

Contents

Preface

This book was first published exactly 20 years ago, in May 1994. It sold in many thousands of copies. It was written for, and seemed to speak to, an audience created by the struggles of the preceding four years. These included the anti-poll tax campaign which destroyed not only the Tory government's flagship policy but also, ultimately, Margaret Thatcher's all too long premiership. They also included the revolt against the 1992 pit closure programme which involved two huge protest marches in central London. One of these was the biggest march on a working day until, a decade or so later, the Stop the War Coalition protest at George Bush's visit to London in 2003. In addition there were strikes in the health service, marches and meetings to oppose the first Gulf War, and a movement against the Criminal Justice Bill.

In a longer timescale the book could look back on about a decade and a half of neo-liberal economics, if we take the previous welfare state/Keynesian consensus to have been abandoned when the Labour government of the late 1970s accepted the International Monetary Fund cuts programme.

In the 20 years since then practically every indicator of working class living standards has changed for the worse: inequality is greater, infant mortality is worse; real wages have declined, welfare provision is meaner; the cost of education is greater, the chance of a stable job much reduced; pensioners are poorer, workers less likely to enjoy the protection of union membership.

But there have been some notable, in some cases historic, movements of resistance. The global anti-capitalist movement which began with mass demonstrations against the World Trade Organisation in Seattle in 1999 was a signal event. It brought together climate change and environmental activists with trade union demonstrators— the famous teamster-turtle alliance. It named the enemy in the most general political terms: capitalism. And it self-identified as an 'anti-capitalist' movement. This was new. I remember watching the BBC main news bulletin where the commentator said 'anti-capitalist protestors took over the centre of Seattle today'. I'd rarely heard the BBC use the word 'capitalist', let alone the words 'anti-capitalist' before. This term became the hallmark of many demonstrations to this day. It had a great strength: an immediate identification of the entire system as the problem. But there was also a corresponding weakness: a much lower level of direct workplace struggle than in the 1968-1975 period.

Even so the movement's political strength became greater as the anti-war movement arose, involving many of the same forces, in response to the invasions of Afghanistan and Iraq in 2002-2003. Again, just as the anti-capitalist movement had popularised to millions of ordinary citizens language once the exclusive property of the left, so the rise of the mass anti-war movement made anti-imperialism a mass popular force on a scale that even exceeded that achieved by the anti-Vietnam protests. At the same time, and partly as a consequence, establishment politics became hollowed out to an unprecedented degree. Faced with mainstream parties all of whom embraced neo-liberalism at home and defended imperialism abroad the old system began to crack. Political party membership fell and turnout in elections declined. Opinion polls revealed that public faith in politicians, the police, the media and other pillars of the status quo were at historic lows.

And yet at the same time the organisation of the left was also facing a crisis. The Labour Left has probably never been weaker. The Communist Party left is much reduced after the body blow of the East European revolutions of 1989, far longer and deeper in their effect on the left than many thought at the time. The revolutionary far left has, in all too many cases, retreated into sectarian isolation.

In fact the central paradox of left politics can be formulated in this way: at a time when an unprecedented level of ideological radicalism have seized large sections of the working class the far left has been unable to strengthen itself because it is wedded to 1970s models of industrial militancy which prevents it from understanding the tasks before it.

This is not to deny, of course, that workplace struggle is a central component of any project for working class liberation. But when such resistance is at low levels it is the height of foolishness not to use the radicalism that does exist as a lever to get us closer to the radicalism we need.

In short, the existing left is not in danger from 'liquidating' itself under the rightward pressure of ordinary workers. On the contrary, the left is not 'too close' to existing working class consciousness, but too far from it to engage with it effectively. Of course there are many arguments to be had—indeed the very arguments outlined in this book. But they cannot even be begun by a left that is so far distant from its intended audience that they pay it no mind. There are many struggles—against austerity, against war, to strengthen trade unions—in which socialists can engage in common struggle with those they seek to win. But many on the left have forgotten that joint action is always the best place to conduct an argument. They prefer loud-hailer propaganda conducted in self-satisfied, knowing, isolation from the struggles that can be fought now.

This needs to change. To advance we need more socialists, and more socialists who are working together in political organisation. This new edition of The ABC of Socialism will, I hope, help more people become socialists, and help more socialists to become effective organisers.

John Rees
London, May 2014

1. Becoming a socialist

Imagine that a grand parade is about to pass before us. It is a parade of the entire population of Britain and it will last one hour. But there is something strange about this parade, something that will tell us a great deal about the society we live in. The height of the people in the parade is determined by their income—the poor are short, the rich are tall. Imagine that we, the spectators, are the average height—that is the average income for the economy as a whole. Here is what we would witness.

First we see minuscule characters pass by, no taller than a matchstick. They are housewives who have worked for a short time and who have nothing like an annual income. There are school kids with a part time job, FE students still living at home. It takes five minutes for them to pass.

In the next five or six minutes the people passing before us become noticeably taller, but they are still the size of elves, perhaps two or three feet high. They are young people on social security, the unemployed, very many old age pensioners and owners of small shops doing poor trade. Next come a wide range of low paid workers: young nurses, lower grade civil servants, refuse collectors. The unskilled white collar workers march in front of the unskilled manual workers. A sizeable proportion of Britain's black and Asian population is passing before us now.

It takes 15 minutes for the marchers to reach a height much over four feet. For us this is a disturbing sight. Fifteen minutes is a long time to see people march by who barely reach our waist. Nor is there much relief in sight. Another 10 minutes goes by before small people who reach our collar bone arrive on the scene—skilled manual workers, office workers with considerable training. We know the parade will last an hour and perhaps we expected that after half an hour we would be able to look the marchers in the eye, but we are still looking down on the top of their heads and even in the far distance there is no sign of improvement. The height is growing terribly slowly. A full three quarters of an hour has passed before we see people our own size arriving.

But in the last ten minutes, with the arrival of the top 10 percent, the parade becomes sensational. At first they are modestly tall, perhaps six feet six inches: headmasters, department heads—people who never thought they were in the top 10 percent. Then things become really bizarre.

Giants loom over us: a not particularly successful lawyer—18 feet tall. The first doctors come into view—24 feet high. The first accountants, taller even than the doctors. There is still a minute to go. Now we see figures far bigger than houses: a university professor 27 feet high, senior managers in large firms 30 feet high, a permanent secretary in Whitehall 40 feet tall and even taller high court judges. Top accountants and surgeons go past at a height of 60 feet or more.

Even this is not the end of it. Now the sun is blotted out by figures the size of tower blocks. Most of them are businessmen, managers of large firms and holders of many directorships, some are film stars or members of the royal family. Prince Philip is 180 feet high. John Paul Getty's height is incalculable—at least ten miles high, perhaps twice that.

This description is now more than 40 years old. It comes from a book by economist Jan Pen. I was at school when I first read it. If the parade were to march again today, the poor would be very considerably smaller, the rich even taller.

Thinking about what caused such inequality, and knowing that my parents would be near the start of that parade, was one thing that first set me wondering about socialism. But it was only one part of a mosaic, fragments of which came from books while others came from my own experience.

I remember trying to get the school authorities to agree to a school council. I couldn't see, and still can't, why the people who are being educated, the people for whom the school is supposed to exist, shouldn't have a say in its running. I remember walking to a youth club in the pitch black caused by the power cuts during the 1974 miners' strike. And I can still remember the disappointment of reading, not long after, that Tony Benn had been replaced as industry minister by right winger Eric Varley, ending what I saw as experiments in workers' control.

I searched for something that would get me a little further than that passage in Jan Pen's text book. I tried Marx and Engels' Communist Manifesto. I have read and re-read it many times since and each time get more out of it. But back then it was the wrong book at the wrong time, written in a language with which I could not get to grips. Eventually, I read George Orwell's magnificent book about the 1936 Spanish Revolution, Homage to Catalonia. His description of revolutionary Barcelona convinced me that workers could make a revolution:

> *It was the first time that I had ever been in a town where the working class was in the saddle. Practically every building of any size had been seized by the workers and was draped with red flags or with the red and black flags of the Anarchists; every wall was scrawled with the hammer and sickle and with the initials of the revolutionary parties... Every shop and cafe had an inscription saying that it had been collectivised; even the bootblacks had been collectivised and boxes painted red and black. Waiters and shop-walkers looked you in the eye and treated you as an equal... In outward existence it was a town in which the wealthy classes had ceased to exist. Practically everyone wore rough working class clothes, or blue overalls, or some*

variant of the militia uniform. All this was queer and moving. There is much in it that I did not understand, in some ways I did not even like it, but I recognised it immediately as a state of affairs worth fighting for.

So now I knew what I was for and what I was against. But there was so much more I still didn't know. Was the Labour Party socialist? If it wasn't, what kind of organisation should socialists join? What about the unions, or women's liberation? What kind of arguments could you use against racism?

Most working class people become socialists in this way. A bit of direct experience, a bit of general experience added to a bit of reading about politics, class and socialist history. I wish that at some point during those years someone had pushed a little book into my hand to speed up the whole process, make things clearer and suggest a course of action. This book is designed to do that for a new generation of socialists.

2. Why the working class?

People become socialists because they want to end poverty, injustice, exploitation and oppression. But how can this be done?

The rich seem to have endless resources to protect their power. In the board rooms of Tesco and Nissan, of BP and Shell, of MacAlpine and McDonald's, they decide the what and when, the quantity and the quality, of production. They decide how many workers will work, how much they will be paid, how long and how hard their day will be. Finally, they decide the price we have to pay for the goods we have produced.

But the rich own much more than the factories, offices, banks and transport firms. They also own the great ideas factories—the newspaper and TV companies, the internet companies and film studios which promote and pay commentators who flatter the prejudices of the wealthy.

Beyond even this, the relatives and acquaintances of the rich, the friends from public schools and West End clubs, control those parts of the establishment where private ownership is excluded. So, the heads of the civil service, the executives of the BBC, the high court judges, the chief constables and high ranking military officers share the values and interests of the privately wealthy. Even this thin distinction has been much eroded recently. Private business is increasingly directly represented in every sphere from the committees which run schools to sponsorship of the Royal Shakespeare Company.

This is why the wealthy are more than just a group of people with a lot of money. More importantly, they also own the means of producing wealth which, in turn, gives them economic and political power. It also gives the rich shared interests opposed to those of other groups in society. Together ownership and power, and the common values and wealth that these make possible, mean that the rich form a ruling class.

But for all the power of the ruling class, there is one group in society whose power is potentially as great—the working class. This comprises the vast majority of people who cannot survive unless they sell their labour in return for a wage. Without workers' labour, manual and mental, nothing moves. The power station turbine stands silent, the production line shudders to a halt, the computer screen goes dark, the superstore's shelves remain empty and the banking transaction collapses. This is the great weakness of the ruling class. They may own the great factories, offices, media corporations, shops and banks—but without us these properties are so many empty hulks. Without us the great money-making machines of the rich stand idle.

Some people say the working class is shrinking. But they only look at the falling number of manual workers in Britain's traditional industries like coal mining or ship building, or at the big job losses in manufacturing industry. They forget that manual workers are still a third of the British workforce, and they never see that great swathes of the working class in offices and huge, factory-like stores and call centres now suffer the same hours, boredom and pay as production line workers.

The ruling class, of course, would like 'labour saving' machines to do our work. But they can never do without us because every technical advance—from the steam engine to the smart phone—has itself to be made by workers. So today the working class is much bigger than it was 100 years ago, both in this country and worldwide.

Not only is the working class still with us, but it is also still fighting. Indeed, the history of the last century is punctuated with great revolutionary outbursts by workers: the 1905 revolution in Russia, the two great revolutions of 1917 in Russia, the German Revolution of 1918, the British

General Strike of 1926, the Spanish Revolution of 1936, the Hungarian revolution of 1956, the Czechoslovakian uprising and the French general strike of 1968, the Portuguese Revolution of 1974, the rise of Solidarity in Poland in 1981—to mention only some of the most famous. Even the 1989 East European revolutions, especially in Romania and Czechoslovakia, would have been impossible without workers' struggles, even though workers have gained little from them. And in the twenty-first century the great wave of Arab Revolutions that began in 2010 demonstrated, whatever the difficulties those revolts have subsequently encountered, that the modern capitalist system can still face revolutionary challenges from those it rules.

In Britain the recent decades have been difficult ones for the workers' movement, but it is not true that workers gave up fighting. The Great Miners Strike of 1984-85 was the longest mass strike in European history. There were also hard fought battles by printers, seafarers, hospital workers, steel workers and dockers. And recently the long decline of trade union membership has begun to be reversed. And when you look back over the fate of four of the last six British prime ministers you can see why the British ruling class has fought so hard to break the power of the workers' movement. Tory Edward Heath's anti union laws were smashed by the threat of a general strike in 1972 and Heath lost office in the wake of the miners' strike of 1974. Labour's James Callaghan took on the firefighters and then council workers and other public sector workers in the 1979 Winter of Discontent. He failed to hold down wages and then lost the subsequent election. Even Margaret Thatcher, the Iron Lady herself, was eventually forced from office by the overwhelmingly working class anti poll tax movement. Tony Blair survived in office but his reputation was forever destroyed by the mass opposition he faced over his decision to go to war in Afghanistan and Iraq.

There will be plenty more struggles in the future because capitalism is a system which drives workers to fight back. This is how. To survive, each boss has to avoid being beaten by his competitors: So every capitalist tries to get his workers to work longer and harder in return for less than his competitors can. Competition forces each individual capitalist to attack the jobs, wages and conditions of workers. Because this pattern is repeated in every firm it results in a struggle between the whole class of capitalists and the class of workers.

Inevitably workers resist because their very livelihood is at risk. They form unions, protest and go on strike as they have done from capitalism's very earliest days. Sometimes such revolts are small and local, sometimes they assume the scale of a mass movement, a general strike or a revolution. So just as the ruling class try day in, day out to weaken the workers' movement, socialists seek to defend and strengthen it.

No other group in society, no other class, has the same power to defeat the ruling class, or the same interest in seeing the ruling class defeated. No other group can stop the flow of wealth to the ruling class and paralyse the institutions of government, simply by stopping work. No other group has the same level of organisation or the same history of continuous struggle against the system.

3. How do ideas change?

Workers have the power to make a revolution—but will they use it? Certainly a revolution will never happen unless large numbers of workers are convinced of the need for it. The success of a revolution depends on it being 'a movement of the immense majority, in the interests of the immense majority', as Karl Marx and Frederick Engels wrote in the Communist Manifesto. Yet most workers, most of the time, are far from revolutionary.

Simply arguing revolutionary ideas with them, or getting them to read a website like Counterfire, while it convinces an important minority, will not convince the majority.

Fortunately, workers' life experience often politicises them before they meet a revolutionary socialist.

Consider what, at minimum, happens when workers strike. The mind numbing tedium of the daily routine is shattered. No longer under the thumb of the supervisor, no longer told what to do, when to do it and how fast to do it, strikers begin to take their lives into their own hands. Instead of being isolated from one another and made to feel they are a tiny cog in a very big machine, workers begin to see that, collectively, they are very powerful. Their confidence begins to rise.

Perhaps initially the strikers may believe that as soon as the boss hears their case, as soon as the manager listens to reason, the union will be able to achieve some or all of its demands. Strikers may believe that the press will report the strike fairly and that if the police or courts become involved they will act in an unbiased fashion. The direct experiences of generations of strikers have taught them differently: wage cuts and sackings do not happen because bosses are ill informed or because they make illogical judgments—bosses do it to make a profit and avoid being forced into bankruptcy by their competitors. So they are unlikely to be moved no matter how compelling the union's case. The media are not neutral—they are owned by big business and, 99 times out of 100, they take the side of business. The courts and the police are biased in labour disputes.

Obviously, the bigger the dispute the more deeply the ideas of those involved will be transformed. A one day strike in a small local workplace will not have the same impact as the Great Miners' Strike of 1984-85. A strike that is lost will not radicalise to the same degree as a strike that ends in victory. And although strike action often transforms workers' ideas faster and more completely than anything else, it certainly isn't the only way political consciousness is transformed. Participation in a rent strike or a student occupation, in a mass movement like the anti poll tax campaign or the anti-war movement can often have a similar effect.

The more directly involved workers are in such campaigns the more likely they are to begin to see the whole system through different eyes. But the beginnings of such changes in consciousness can often be underway long before workers begin to move. To be disciplined at work, even if no strike results; to be suddenly forced to pay more tax or rent or child maintenance, even if no campaign takes place; to see a series of miscarriages of justice exposed, even if you personally are not involved, can all begin the process of politicisation. In this way life itself can begin to transform workers' ideas. At work, in the home, in the wider society, the class nature of the system forces its way into the minds of people who perhaps would not otherwise think of themselves as political at all.

'Workers become political when they have to fight the government for a crust of bread', said the Russian revolutionary, Vladimir Lenin. He did not mean that workers must be literally starving before they begin to think of revolution. He meant that when the most basic necessities— a job, a decent wage, a place to live, health and education systems—are denied to workers, when they have to fight to defend these things not just in this factory or that town, but in every workplace and city in the country, then political consciousness begins to take root. That consciousness grows most quickly when workers not only have a burning desire to put a stop to all the bad things that are happening in their lives, but when they also begin to take action to do something about realising that desire.

Then they begin to see what is wrong with society, how all the forces of the ruling class—the media, the police, the government—act against them. And, as the organisational strength of workers grows, so they become more confident and more imaginative in their ideas about the possibility of socialism. The capacity to think more daring thoughts grows out of every act of solidarity, every strike that is won, every campaign that succeeds, every racist who is humiliated. Then the path is open for socialist arguments to find an audience of millions instead of thousands, a path opened up by workers' direct experience of class society and the realities of the struggle against it.

4. Why socialists are trade unionists

The working class does not have its own police force, neither does it command the pen of national newspaper editors, nor the ear of the high court judges and senior civil servants. But it does have two great strengths: its numbers and its economic power, the power to stop production.

Those strengths can only be used if workers unite—and unity requires organisation. The preconditions for such unity and organisation are partly provided by the way capitalism itself works.

In our society workers are brought together in huge cities and set to work in massive workplaces. They work and live side by side and experience broadly similar living standards. This was not always true. Peasants, who did the work in medieval society, were scattered across the countryside. There were often great differences in wealth between rich and poor peasants. When they had a grievance they would sometimes unite briefly in a riot, but they could never build stable organisations.

Workers, precisely because capitalism brings them together in great numbers in similar conditions, have always defended themselves collectively by building collective organisations—unions. Indeed, the very first unions built by workers in Britain 200 years ago were called 'combinations' and the very first anti union laws, passed soon afterwards, were called the Combination Acts.

Union organisation, now as then, is a great step forward. To see what a difference the union makes you only have to compare the wages of unionised and non-unionised workers in Britain. On average unionised workers are 10 percent better off. It's the same internationally. US workers, where unionisation is low, have suffered a much sharper fall in living standards than workers in Britain who, even now, are better unionised.

Anyone who has worked in a non-union workplace knows how confident the bosses are: how they alter hours and wages at will, and victimise anyone who objects, how they cut corners on health and safety, enforce zero hours contracts, and sack people without notice. Being in a union, by contrast, makes workers feel more confident. They can force managers to deal with them collectively, not single them out. They can elect shop stewards and officials who can negotiate with management. They have an organisation with funds and links with other workers so that if they take action they have a chance of financial and practical help. In a union workers learn how to organise, how to argue, how to reach a democratic decision and see that it is carried out. Being in a union helps workers to see themselves as a class, to see they have more in common with other workers than they do with the boss or the government.

All this can happen even before the union takes any action. But when the union does take action, all these strengths become even more important.

In a strike workers see that union organisation is essential for effective, united action; that pickets are ineffective without organisation; that union members are less likely to cross a picket line; that union members are more likely to give to a strike fund and more likely to take solidarity action. And because in the course of the struggle to build and defend the unions workers see that the press, police, courts and the rest of the establishment nearly always side with the employers, union members are more likely to be socialists.

But, to be effective the union must include all workers, socialist or not. The union is the basic defence organisation of the working class. Its primary function is to secure the things that every worker needs—a job, a good wage, safe conditions and decent hours. This all-inclusive unity, organised around the most basic issues which all workers have in common, is the secret of union power. 'Unity is strength' as the old slogan says.

But the strength of the unions can also be a weakness, especially when it comes to anything more than fighting to defend wages and conditions. Unions fight for better conditions under capitalism, not to end capitalism. Unions fight the bosses so that they will give workers better wages and conditions, not to get rid of the bosses once and for all. Unions ask for a bigger slice of the cake, not the whole bakery.

In some battles this weakness may not be decisive. To win this wage claim or to stop that victimisation may be possible whether you believe that the boss will always be there or whether you think that workers can run society without bosses. But in other struggles, especially very big battles like the 1926 General Strike or the Great Miners' Strike, union organisation alone is not enough. Why not?

These disputes began over trade union issues— jobs, conditions and wages—but the implications of defeat or victory for both sides meant that much more was at stake. If the miners had beaten Thatcher, the whole balance of forces would have swung in favour of the working class. If the General Strike had been victorious the government would have collapsed and Britain would have faced the beginnings of a revolutionary crisis.

When the stakes are so high the bosses and the government recognise that they are no longer dealing with mere economic grievances or trade union questions. They realise that the whole structure of society could be swept away. At such times, if the working class does not go beyond simple trade unionism and develop a political strategy which can answer the question, 'Who should run society, workers or capitalists?' they will be at a massive disadvantage.

If workers lose such struggles, if they don't press beyond trade union issues to the political issue of who runs society, the ruling class can stabilise its position. Then it will wreak a terrible revenge, as it did after the General Strike and the

Great Miners' Strike. This is why, in really big struggles, workers not only stick to their union but also look to socialist parties to struggle on a political and economic level, raising the question, 'Who runs society?' When the ruling class realises its very existence is at stake and fights accordingly, the outcome of the struggle depends on workers building a revolutionary organisation which can confront the bosses in this way.

Politics is important even in small disputes. It may not be crucial for the whole working class whether a strike wins or loses, but it is vital for the strikers and it can be important for the workers' movement locally. Sometimes such disputes can assume national significance. In these disputes Labour MPs and union officials argue that a 'public relations' campaign, lobbying councillors and MPs and trusting the union officials is the key to victory—just as in big conflicts they urge workers to obey the law, trust the TUC and not dabble in 'politics'.

Revolutionary socialists will argue differently. They stress the importance of rank and file activity, of workers electing their own strike committee to lead the dispute, of picketing and solidarity from other workers even if that means breaking the anti union laws—just as in bigger struggles they urge workers not to rely on the established leaders, to build workers' councils and to dare to run society themselves.

On the one hand, in a revolution or a local dispute we have the bureaucrats' old cry, 'Stay within the law and leave it to us,' on the other, the revolutionaries' watchword, 'The self activity of workers is the key to victory.'

5. Why do the union leaders sell out?

Why on Earth would the leader of the public sector union Unison call off action against the government's plans to axe his members pensions at the very moment that struggle had mobilised half a million workers on a demonstration in 2012? Why did the then leader of the Trades Union Congress, Norman Willis, in October 1992 when the plans to close most of the mining industry were announced, tell millions of trade unionists who were willing to take action to get rid of the government that what was needed was a 'cooling off period'?

Why did the leaders of all the major unions stand by and watch the miners go down to defeat in the Great Miners' Strike of 1984-85 when just a little solidarity action would have finished off Thatcher's government?

One reason why union leaders are like this lies in the nature of unions themselves. A strong union is, by definition, a relatively stable, well organised institution. It necessarily has structures and routines built up over time. In all but exceptional circumstances, most of its members, most of the time, will not be engaged in any industrial action. This inevitably produces inertia at all levels. But union leaders embody this conservatism much more fully than the rank and file.

An ordinary union member will take industrial action sometimes. The full time union official never takes action. The wages or the job of the ordinary worker depends on the union taking action, often action which risks union funds. The officials, because they are paid by the union, are often fearful if anything disrupts the normal bureaucratic functioning of the union, particularly if there is any legal or financial risk involved.

Everything about union officials' lives assures them that they are different, and superior, to ordinary workers. They no longer work the same hours and shifts, are no longer dependent on the bosses for a job and enjoy wages and conditions far better than the members of the union. To go with this different position in life, union officials develop a hardened set of ideas which no struggle, no matter how powerful, will ever totally wipe away. They believe gradual change, compromise and negotiation are the only ways to settle anything. The Labour Party is therefore their natural political home.

Of course many workers are supporters of the Labour Party as well, and often share some of the ideas of the union officials. But strikes and other struggles affect ordinary union members much more sharply than they do union officials. The most basic necessities of workers' lives depend on the outcome of such struggles. Union officials' lives go on much the same whether these struggles win or lose—the UNISON officials still have their jobs and wage increases, no matter what happens to the workers in the hospitals.

However, more important than all this is the fact that the union officials' whole function in life is one of negotiating with the bosses on behalf of workers. If workers begin to take on the bosses by themselves, if they decide they can best get what they want not by quietly paying their dues and leaving the talking to the official, but by taking strike action, then the whole purpose of the union officials' life is called into question. Indeed, the bigger the struggle, the more dramatic the divide between union leaders and the rank and file becomes. For ordinary workers a general strike or a revolution raises the prospect of a better life, for the union officials it represents a threat to their privileged life. For these reasons the key division in the unions is between the rank and file and the full time union officials.

So union leaders are different from the rank and file, but

that doesn't mean they are the same as the bosses. Union leaders do not own factories, sack workers or cut wages. They may be reluctant to call strikes, but sometimes they do. No employer ever called a strike. Many union leaders may be right wing Labour Party members, but they are not Tories. That union leaders' livelihoods ultimately depend on the union, not the employer, is a double-edged weapon. It means they are removed from the pressure of the day to day struggle, but also that they need the union to survive.

The union officials are not a class, either of owners like the bosses or of workers like the rank and file. The union officials are an in-between layer. They often sell out as a result of pressure from the bosses. But they can also be pushed into action by the rank and file, providing the pressure is strong enough.

Of course, not all union officials are the same.

The national union leader is often further removed from the pressure of the rank and file than the local official. A left wing union leader is obviously preferable to some dyed in the wool right winger—if only because the rank and file may have more room for action under a left winger. And many left-wing union leaders are elected because rank and file members want change but are not always confident enough to take action themselves. But even the local left winger will only move if he or she is pushed from below, otherwise pressure from the bosses and the union hierarchy will win out.

6. What is rank and file organisation?

Where rank and file trade unionists find themselves faced with a stubbornly entrenched layer of full-time officials they often react by creating organisations of their own which can more fully and immediately represent their interests. These are directly elected bodies, based on the workplace. The delegates can be immediately recalled and still work at the same job as those who elect them, unlike the union officials. The closest parallels in the trade union movement today are the shop stewards' committees in some workplaces. The geographical trade union branch and the local trades council are both more cut off from the mass of workers, less able to organise them for action and less responsive to their needs.

Today's shop steward committees are a faint echo of the mass rank and file movements that have existed in the past—the Shop Stewards' and Workers' Committee Movement of the First World War or the Minority Movement built by the Communist Party in the 1920s. Indeed, current shop stewards' organisation is still much weaker than it was in the early 1970s. These, in turn, were not as strong as the earlier movements on which they were modelled. A relatively high level of struggle was necessary for these organisations to flourish. A low level of struggle neither sufficiently radicalises a section of the rank and file, nor does it create a network of local militants who can build an organisation to provide an alternative leadership to the officials.

This does not mean that at present there is no antagonism between rank and file militants and the officials. There is, and it expresses itself particularly sharply when strikes occur. Nor does it mean that there is no such thing as a rank and file strategy: in every struggle such a strategy means encouraging the self activity of workers— for active picketing, approaching other workers for solidarity, electing a strike committee and arguing against the passivity of relying on the officials, MPs or the media.

But it does mean that national rank and file organisation, capable of calling action independently of the officials, does not exist at the moment.

When such struggles do exist the vitality and confidence that floods into rank and file organisations, often originating as strike committees, is unmistakable. Thousands of militants begin to have the faith that they can call action if the officials sell them short. As the famous declaration of the Clyde Workers' Committee in 1915 said:

> We will support the officials so long as they rightly represent the workers, but we will act independently immediately they misrepresent them. Being composed of delegates from every shop and untrammelled by the obsolete rule of law, we claim to represent the true feelings of the workers. We can act immediately according to the merits of the case and the desire of the rank and file.

This statement brims with the confidence of militants who had already led mass strikes in the most difficult wartime conditions in the teeth of opposition from the employers, the state and the union leaders. They were so successful that they built a rank and file movement across the usual occupational divides and union demarcations that criss-cross the working class. They were, therefore, half way between traditional trade unionism, which fights over economic issues with a particular boss or group of bosses, and an organisation like a workers' council, which unites the entire working class and challenges the political and economic power of the ruling class as a whole.

Similarly, the rank and file papers produced by the Communist Party in the 1920s sold tens of thousands of copies to workers who had broken, or partly broken, with the trade union leaders but were not yet in full political agreement with revolutionary socialists. The rank and file movements could advance the struggle in a way that a revolutionary party alone could not have the forces to do. In the heat of such struggles, the rank and file movements provided a forum for discussion between revolutionaries and non-revolutionaries and an arena where non-revolutionaries could see in practice the worth of revolutionary organisation.

Rank and file organisation, therefore, provides a way for all militants, revolutionary and non-revolutionary, to increase their weight in the union and in the struggle by trying to promote the maximum self activity and organisation by the mass of union members.

This aim distinguishes rank and file organisation from two other strategies which union activists have sometimes tried to use to combat the officials. Sometimes militants become so frustrated with officials and so despairing of ordinary workers' willingness to fight that they split off to form unions of their own. An echo of this frustration is sometimes found today among workers influenced by autonomist political strategies. These 'red unions' are nearly always a disaster because they separate the militants from the very rank and file they wish to influence. Nothing pleases a right wing union leader more than to see the best militants lose patience and cut themselves off from their fellow workers. This was the reaction of Eric Hammond, the deeply right wing leader of the electricians union who organised a scab workforce to start up Rupert Murdoch's Wapping printing plant in 1986, when some of the militants in the union split away to form their own union in the late 1980s.

The second mistaken reaction is for militants to think if only they were elected as a union leader they would be much more radical. This electoralist strategy has been the organising principle of the Broad Lefts in the unions over many years. And of course it has one very powerful argument in its favour: it is always better to elect a left-winger or militant than to allow the right wing to gain control of a union. And in the absence of the conditions where rank and file organisation can be built this strategy becomes even more attractive.

The trouble is, even on those occasions a left winger who sticks to their principles gets elected, what they can do is severely circumscribed unless the members are organised below them to win the argument for action in every office and workshop where the union has members.

Arthur Scargill, who did stick to his principles during the 1984-85 miners' strike, was nevertheless powerless to organise solidarity for the miners outside the control of the TUC leaders because there was no network of militants, either among the miners or among other workers, to organise independently of the union officials. The longer Scargill continued at the top of the union without such a base, the more he became a prisoner of the union leaders. So it was that in the 1992 pit crisis he didn't break decisively with the TUC's 'do nothing' public opinion strategy.

This does not mean, of course, that socialists don't care whether left-wingers like Len McCluskey or Mark Serwotka, rather than a right winger, heads a union. We'd obviously fight to have the left winger. But such election victories can only have any real meaning for the mass of ordinary workers if they are part of building a rank and file organisation. In the case of the Broad Lefts historically, however, electoralism is an alternative to rank and file organisation. So although socialists often need to be part of the Broad Lefts during times when it is impossible to build rank and file movements, we always seek to advance a rank and file strategy and to combat electoralist tendencies.

7. Was Labour ever socialist?

Most people today wonder whether there are really any major policy differences between Labour leaders and the Tories. But was there a golden past? Was Labour ever a socialist party?

Certainly the Labour Party had more socialists in it before the Kinnock purges of the 1980s. And Labour Party members, even Labour leaders, were once happier to use the word socialism than they are today. Labour, after all, was born out of the trade unions early this century. But the unavoidable fact is that most Labour leaders have never liked working class struggle. As soon as they got into government, they were desperate to convince the establishment that it would do nothing to damage the capitalist system.

Ramsey MacDonald, Labour's first prime minister, came to office at the head of a minority government in 1924. It was a time of high unemployment and sharp class polarisation. A few years earlier 30 Labour councillors from the London borough of Poplar had been jailed for refusing to surrender money they thought should be spent on the poor. MacDonald surveyed this scene and spelled out what kind of 'socialism' Labour stood for:

Public doles, Poplarism, strikes for increased wages, limitations of output are not only not Socialism but may mislead the spirit and the policy of Socialism.

When dockers struck in February 1924 MacDonald told them:

The government will not fail to take the steps necessary to secure transport and food supplies, and has already set up the nucleus of an organisation.

Indeed, the Labour government had inherited brutal and authoritarian means from its Tory predecessor in the form of the Emergency Powers Act and secret plans to combat a general strike. The Labour minister responsible didn't alter the plans, handing them back to the next Tory government with the words:

> I haven't destroyed any of your plans, in fact I haven't done a bloody thing with them.

The Tories used the plans to break the 1926 General Strike. The first Labour government had certainly been, in the words of one of its members, 'a national government not a class government'.

The dreary pattern has been repeated ever since. In 1931 MacDonald split the Labour Party over the issue of cutting unemployment benefit. He and other leading Labour Party figures joined the Tory government. Labour's right wing has always been happier to undermine the party than see it challenge the status quo. The 'Gang of Four'—Shirley Williams, David Owen, Roy Jenkins and William Rodgers—all former Labour ministers, did the same in the 1980s when they formed the SDP. The resulting split in the Labour vote was the main electoral reason why Thatcher stayed in power. But most of the time, Labour's right wing don't have to split in order to get their own way—usually the left are either too weak to oppose, or go along with, the right's plans.

Even the best Labour government of all time, the 1945 administration that brought in the welfare state and the National Health Service, confirms the old pattern in some very significant ways. Labour was elected by a landslide, but Labour leader Clement Attlee's ministers sent troops against striking meat porters, lorry drivers, engineers and boilermakers, dockers, power station workers and gas maintenance workers. Attlee was also secretly developing the nuclear bomb, without even telling the cabinet, and using MI5 against left wingers. Even the health service was not a specifically socialist policy. It was planned by Sir William Beveridge, a Liberal, and would have been introduced even if the Tories had been returned in 1945, albeit in a less generous form.

In fact the NHS, like nationalisation and other welfare reforms, was only possible for three reasons, none of which had much to do with the Labour's socialist intentions. Firstly, the nationalised war economy had laid the basis for many of the measures which were to be institutionalised under Labour. Secondly, the capitalist system was expanding and so could afford reform. Thirdly, the ruling class was afraid that the post war popular demand for change might spill over into revolution. This was the era when arch Tory Quintin Hogg, later Lord Hailsham, warned:

> *Give them social reform, or they will give you social revolution.*

Labour were out of office in 1951 and didn't get back in until 1964, by which time the long post war boom was beginning to fade. The more it faded, the more Labour turned on its supporters. It broke the seamen's strike in 1966, the year of its re-election, and drew up the blueprint for the first anti union laws, 'In Place Of Strife', but was forced to back down in the face of union protests. Out of office again in 1970, the same story continued when two Wilson-Callaghan governments were returned between 1974 and 1979. Now the crisis was really beginning to bite and Labour made the first cuts in education, the first cuts in NHS spending, increased prescription charges and stood by as unemployment soared to over one million.

The cuts and a pay freeze eventually produced a fight with public sector unions. The government had already made itself unpopular during the struggle with the fire-fighters when the army was used to try and break the strike, and now it fell as a consequence of the 1979 Winter of Discontent. Labour had so disgusted its natural supporters, so abused the idea of socialism, that Margaret Thatcher's Tories seemed like an alternative to a minority of workers. That minority of workers, along with the Tories' natural supporters, tipped the balance and were enough to get her into office.

That Labour government paved the way for Thatcherism because it repeated the mistake of its precursors—it tried to run capitalism better than the Tories. And New Labour under Tony Blair institutionalised the belief that Labour should differ only in fine detail from Tory economic orthodoxy.

8. Why does Labour fail?

Ask most Labour supporters why the party has such a right-wing record and they will probably explain, half apologetically, that because Labour is an electoral party it has no choice but to reflect the views of the voters.

And voters, they say, aren't particularly left-wing.

There is a grain of truth in this argument. Most of the time most workers' ideas are influenced by the newspapers and TV, the education system, establishment press agents and mainstream political parties. These institutions express almost universally conservative ideas, hostile to the very idea of socialism. An electoral party, which doesn't organise the militant minority of workers as a way of influencing the combativity and consciousness of the whole class, ends up at least partially reinforcing conservative ideas, not challenging them.

But electoralism is only part of the story. There are times when even the middle of the road consciousness among workers is to the left of the Labour Party. This has been the case since the revolt against the poll tax and the fall of Thatcher, and it became even more true as Tony Blair drove Labour even further to the right.

Today, and on many of these previous occasions, Labour's electoral chances would improve if it showed more fight. So why is it so rare for Labour to run with the tide when the tide runs to the left?

The answer lies in Labour's politics. The Labour Party is founded on the belief that capitalism is here to stay. It was built by the trade union leaders and it shares their view that there may be an improvement here, a reform there, but there can be no thought of workers themselves taking control of society. The market is here to stay. So when the system can afford a little change, Labour may be willing to implement it. But when the system can't afford to give more, Labour acts for the system, not for the workers. Labour is a 'capitalist workers' party'—a party supported by and voted for by workers but which has no greater ambition than to run capitalism according to the system's own rules. Inevitably this means it ends up implementing anti union laws, regressive taxes, and making cuts in hospitals and schools.

Many Labour Party members don't like this at all. Many are socialists and want to change the party. But all attempts to change Labour from the inside show that it is the left who get changed, not Labour Party leadership. Stafford Cripps started out a socialist, tried to change the Labour Party, and ended up a right winger in the 1930s. The same thing happened to Aneurin Bevan in the 1940s and to Michael Foot in the 1970s. Tony Benn tried again in the 1980s but even he failed and his legacy as an uncompromising socialist depends as much on what he did in spite of Labour's leaders, not because of them.

Some socialists agree that the Labour Party is useless for the purposes of getting socialism and an unreliable ally in the day to day struggle and so go on to argue that we shouldn't vote Labour. This is understandable. If there were a better socialist party, even if it weren't a revolutionary party, every socialist would want to vote for it, not Labour. But in the absence of such an alternative, socialists should vote Labour.

The reasons are simple: the Labour Party is not the same as the Tory party. It is not the open representative of big business or funded by big business. Labour may be crippled by its desire to work within the system, but it is funded by the unions and supported by most class conscious workers. In a straight contest between the inadequate, inefficient and cowardly representative of the working class and the all too efficient and brutal representative of the ruling class, socialists should side with the former—while at the same time working to replace it with a socialist alternative.

The people who will build this alternative will be many of the same people who now vote Labour. They will more readily listen to the argument for a socialist alternative if those who are putting it side with Labour against the Tories. Most workers rightly see getting rid of the Tories as a step forward, even if they do not trust Labour. Siding with them against the Tories is the precondition of getting a hearing for our argument about Labour's failings and the need to build a better socialist organisation.

Finally, many workers' faith in the Labour Party cannot be fully broken by argument alone. Direct experience of Labour in power will be a more powerful persuader than the most eloquently argued case against the parliamentary road to socialism. Electing a Labour government is not only a sign that workers reject the openly pro-capitalist Tory party, but also an opportunity for workers to see in practice whether the revolutionaries or the Labour Party leaders were telling the truth about what a Labour government would be like.

Such a combination of argument and experience can win Labour supporters to a revolutionary alternative. When that alternative is large enough it will be able to challenge Labour to a direct struggle for power, a struggle which may involve electioneering for propaganda purposes, but whose main arena will always be the workplaces, the streets and communities.

9. The state

One of the most common objections raised against revolutionaries is that, because we live in a democracy, socialism can be achieved through the existing parliamentary institutions, making revolutionary change unnecessary. Yet one of the most remarkable things about the parliamentary system is how resistant it is to any kind of change, let alone socialism.

One reason for this is that the electoral system favours the Tories. The Tory Party has the massive financial resources of the wealthy at its disposal and nearly unanimous support from the media. Voting takes place secretly and individually, well away from the collective discussions and atmosphere of collective confidence which workers can feel in the workplace and the trade union branch. Even the constituency boundaries have been fixed in such a way that, especially under recent Tory governments, working class areas are attached to middle class areas, diminishing the impact of the working class vote.

But this is not the main reason why the machinery of the state is useless for the purposes of getting socialism.

The vast bulk of the state doesn't even have the flawed and feeble democracy of parliamentary elections. Indeed, most of the state is utterly undemocratic. No one elects the people who run the NHS or the education system, the judges, the civil servants, the police chiefs, the House of Lords, the army officers, the prison governors, the heads of MI5 and MI6 or the directors of public corporations. Nobody even elects the head of state, the queen, although we certainly pay for her lavish lifestyle.

Yet these institutions have far more control over our lives than most MPs. They interpret laws and make regulations, influence benefit levels and prison sentencing policies, determine the price of a stamp or the number of jobs in the building or rail industries, often without telling the government minister responsible. When a minister is consulted, even on the rare occasions that he or she might have a difference of opinion with the civil servants, the officials can bamboozle and cajole the minister into agreement.

The truth is that it is not parliament, not even the cabinet, which runs the state, but the state that runs parliament. The undemocratic triumphs over the democratic part of the machine in nearly every instance.

Even when this fails the ruling class have another card to play—their economic power. The wealthy and the working class can never be politically equal while they are economically unequal. Under capitalism, as the writer Anatole France observed, 'The law leaves everyone equally free to dine at the Ritz or to sleep under Lambeth Bridge'. And it is not just in the case of individual workers that the economic power of the ruling class undermines the formal democracy of parliament.

The same thing happens to government policy. Tony Benn recorded how, as Minister for Energy in the Labour government of the 1970s, he tried to make an agreement with the North Sea oil companies so that they would return a higher than normal amount of the money from North Sea oil to the government. The companies refused. They said that they would not build the rigs, not drill for oil, not pump the oil ashore, not refine it and not transport it to the petrol stations unless they could get the level of profits they wanted.

Tony Benn could beat his chest about being a democratically elected MP and a minister in Her Majesty's Government but ultimately he did not have the power to compel the oil companies to do as he asked.

What happens to individual government policies can also happen to whole governments. Times without number we have seen democratically elected governments—from Harold Wilson's Labour government in the 1960s to Francois Mitterrand's Socialist Party government in the 1980s—drop their reforms in the face of a currency crisis or a crash on the stock exchange.

But what would have happened if Tony Benn had pushed the process one step further? What if Benn had appealed to the workers in the industry to use their power against the oil companies~say by occupying the construction sites and the rigs already built? He would have quickly found that there was another area of the society over which elected politicians have no control: the police and the army.

Every left wing government that has reached this impasse, most famously the Chilean government of Salvador Allende in the early 1970s and Hugo Chavez's government in Venezuela in the last decade, has found that the armed forces turn against their supposed political masters and side with the ruling class. Allende died on the steps of the presidential palace trying to stop an armed forces' coup, Chavez survived but only because a mass popular rising came to his aid.

In all such large scale battles—general strikes and revolutions—the state stands before the working class movement reduced to its bare essentials: the rule of force wielded on behalf of a tiny minority of the rich. The veil of parliament is brushed aside and the rule of the truncheon-wielding policeman, the army strike breaker, the judge who wrongfully imprisons have their day—just as they are doing in the Egyptian counter-revolution today. The Russian revolutionary Lenin was right to say that at the heart of the state lies 'bodies of armed men, prisons etc.'

Workers, unlike Labour Party ministers, do have the power to confront and overcome the power of the state. Strikes can paralyse the civil service and mass demonstrations can be too powerful for even the most determined police force—as the great anti-war demonstrations of the last decade proved. If workers are sufficiently determined they can reduce the police and the army to a state where some of their number defect to the revolution. The rest can be too demoralised and too small, compared with the mass movement, to offer effective resistance. If it seems that the old order is really about to crumble, the old authority of the officers and the hierarchy on which the army and police depend will crumble with it.

But for the workers' movement to be sufficiently determined it needs to be clear that the state machine cannot be reformed, clear that the state must be broken.

Only when workers' own organisations—strike committees, workers' councils, trade unions—are willing and able to take over the running of society will the power of the existing capitalist state be successfully broken. For that, a revolution is necessary.

10. Fighting racism

If you are born black or Asian or are an immigrant in Britain today the facts of life are brutally simple: on average you will be poorer, receive a worse education, live in worse accommodation, find it harder to get a job, be paid less if you do find a job, and are more likely to be insulted or assaulted in the street than if you were born white.

It wasn't always this way. Systematic racism came into the world with the capitalist system. It grew up alongside the slave trade plied between Africa, Europe and America between the 1600s and the 1800s—the very time when capitalism really got a grip on the world economy. This was the age when capitalism developed first in a small number of European states, giving them the wealth to build empires that stretched around the globe.

Slavery and the colonisation of other countries required justification. The ruling class, for the first time in history, began to develop the idea that certain people were inferior solely because of some supposedly inherited 'racial characteristic'. Often—but not always, as the case of anti Irish racism or discrimination against immigrants from eastern Europe shows—this was the colour of a person's skin. It was this 'inferiority' which justified a people being bought and sold and their countries being pillaged by the 'superior' nations.

There have been other forms of discrimination in history. Pre-capitalist societies had discriminated against certain groups on religious or social grounds. The ruling class in ancient Rome thought that all non-Romans were barbarians—but this wasn't a racial characteristic. A Gaul could become a Roman by pledging allegiance to the empire. Equally, ancient Rome was a slave society—but slavery wasn't decided on racial grounds. Slaves, like

Roman emperors, were both black and white. In medieval Europe religious persecution was common—but one could convert to the faith of the rulers and become accepted.

The racism developed by capitalism is more barbaric because, as nationalism and empire grew up, discrimination became an indelible mark associated with race. A black cannot 'convert' into a white and no Jew would imagine that claiming allegiance to the Nazis would stop them from being sent to the concentration camp.

Even after the formal empires which gave rise to racism were destroyed—by two world wars in the twentieth century, and by revolutions in Europe and national liberation struggles in the Third World—racism remained. It is still the crutch supporting every intervention, economic or military, in poorer countries. The language has changed, but not much. Instead of 'dusky natives', we now have 'Palestinian terrorists', instead of 'Zulu cannibals' we have 'Somali warlords', not 'wild Dervishes' but 'Islamic fundamentalists', not 'spear-throwing kaffirs' but 'Latin American drug barons'. The message is the same: the uncivilised 'them' must accept domination by the civilised 'us'. If they don't, there's always the threat of IMF austerity programmes, UN sanctions or US firepower to teach them a lesson.

But there is another reason why racism is still important to capitalism. As capitalism grew it was never simply the case that the major powers intervened from the outside in other countries. They also drew the population of other countries into their own home economies. Racism worked at home to keep these immigrants as second class citizens, paid lower wages, allocated the worst housing and, best of all from our rulers' point of view, dividing and weakening the working class movement.

The British ruling class have been only too happy to see successive generations of workers—Irish, Jews, Afro-Caribbeans and Asians—fill gaps in the labour market, especially when the system is expanding. The King's Speech in 1951 declared, 'My government views with concern the serious shortage of labour, particularly of skilled labour, which has handicapped production in a number of industries'. At about the same time Tory minister Enoch Powell was putting adverts in Caribbean newspapers encouraging workers to come and staff Britain's NHS. But, as the post-war boom faded in the late 1960s and unemployment began to rise, the same Enoch Powell was threatening 'rivers of blood' if black people were allowed into the country.

No working class person has any interest in going along with racist ideas. If racist ideas make it easier for employers to sack a black or Asian worker today, they will find it all the simpler to sack a white worker tomorrow. If employers can pay black or Asian workers low wages, they will use the threat of cheap labour to force all workers to accept lower wages. If immigrants are pushed into slums today, white workers will face the same threat tomorrow.

If black and white workers allow themselves to blame each other for their problems, then united working class resistance to the employers will be all the more difficult to achieve. That is why socialists are absolutely opposed to every sign of racism. That is why we use every opportunity to point out that black and white workers have every interest in joining forces to oppose a system which exploits them both.

Some black activists point to the racism which is still a feature of the Labour Party and parts of the trade union movement as proof that black and white workers cannot unite. They conclude that workers from minority communities must organise separately. Indeed, in many versions of this argument, it is said that all black people, regardless of class, must organise together in separate organisations. Socialists should be happy to defend the right of black people to organise separately, especially in organisations like the Labour Party which have a history of bowing to racist pressure and of supporting racist policies.

But ultimately separatism cannot be a successful strategy for change. It blurs the crucial distinction between black employers and the black middle class on the one hand, and the mass of black workers on the other. The Asian sweatshop owner and the strikers at his plant who want union recognition have less in common than the strikers and the white trade unionists who support their strike fund. The black landlord and the black tenant have less in common than the black and white tenants who both suffer at the landlord's hands. Common union organisation and a common tenants' association will do more for black and white workers than combining black bosses and black workers together in a separate organisation.

This fact becomes even clearer when we look at the battle against capitalism as a whole. Capitalism gave birth to and sustains racism. Black and Asian workers suffer greater oppression than white workers—but they are both oppressed by the same system. The key to ending capitalism and racism is for workers to unite and fight against the system which tries to divide each in order to rule both.

That will not just happen. It will take socialists from all backgrounds to fight every manifestation of racism and so demonstrate that black workers have everything to gain from unity. It will mean black and white workers fighting to overcome the separations that capitalism imposes, not just mirror them in our own organisations.

11. The struggle against fascism

Those who lived through the era of the Holocaust prayed that the nightmare was laid to rest in 1945.

Few people born after the Second World War can have thought they would ever see the rise of mass fascist parties. Yet that is the danger that still persists in the twenty-first century.

In Russia and the former Soviet bloc countries there are powerful fascist movements. In Italy a Mussolini, the granddaughter of the 1930s dictator, has even become an MP. In half a dozen other European countries Nazi parties are stronger than at any time since the Second World War.

Why are the Nazis growing? How big a threat do they pose? What is the best way of stopping them?

The Nazis feed on despair. Where people are worn down by mass unemployment, low wages, homelessness and poor housing, rotting schools and hospital closures, hope is driven out and desperation creeps in. For 20 or 30 years after the Second World War, years dominated by capitalism's longest boom, many people felt that their children's lives would be better than their lives had been. Those hopes have been disappointed in the last 20 years.

Economic disappointment has gone hand in hand with political disillusionment. All the old certainties—about the incorruptibility of the police, the fairness of the courts, the trustworthiness of politicians—are vanishing. Where such traditional ways of life and old values collapse, new ideas will inevitably grow. They can easily be the ideas of the left—as happened in France in the mid-1930s when a strike wave and mass radicalisation defeated the fascists. But the fascists could grow, defeating the left and the workers' movement—as the Nazis did in Germany.

In fact we stand a much better chance of defeating the Nazis today than did the German left of the 1930s. Serious though today's economic crisis is, it is not as deep as the German crisis in the 1930s. In 1932 in Germany there were 8 million unemployed and no unemployment benefit. Today the despair created by the economic crisis is great, but the number unemployed is still lower than in the 1930s—and even with the severe attacks on the level of benefit it is still just enough to keep at bay the kind of desperation felt by German workers in the 1930s.

Neither is the crisis sufficiently deep to drive the mass of the middle class into the arms of the fascists. Hyper-inflation is not wiping out family savings and small businesses are not being driven to the wall in such massive numbers. Middle class despair has not turned into political frenzy, although the rise of UKIP in Britain is a warning that we are not free of such impulses.

The Nazis themselves are still much weaker than in 1930s Germany. By 1930 Hitler could rely on 100,000 stormtroopers, by 1932 that figure had risen to 400,000. Golden Dawn in Greece are beginning to build a base like this but even the biggest Nazi organisations in the rest of Europe have nothing like these forces. They have a degree of electoral support but not yet a comparable fighting force.

Meanwhile, on our side, the level of struggle is much higher than it was in the 1930s—as the strikes and

So the Nazis are not yet as big a threat as they were in the 1930s. *But they can easily continue to grow unless the left takes action to ensure that, when workers break from the old values, they are won to a socialist alternative, not to Nazi reaction.*

To understand how we can stop the Nazis we need to understand what a Nazi organisation is and how it builds its power base. The core of Nazi organisations often comes from the middle classes—be it the traditional middle class of shopkeepers, stall holders and professionals or the new middle class of under-managers, supervisors and foremen. These layers are particularly vulnerable in a social crisis. They have neither the economic power of big business nor the collective power of the unions. They hate the working class which demands more wages and big business which demands a bigger slice of their profits.

The leaders of the British National Party are, like the leaders of the National Front before them, drawn from the lower middle class, just as the leaders of Hitler's Nazis were in the 1930s. But these social layers are not big enough to provide the base for a mass party so, to be effective, the Nazis must draw in wider forces, often from among the most dispossessed and despairing sections of the working class—the permanently unemployed, the destitute and homeless, the Tory voter who works in a small shop or the racist with no union tradition.

This motley collection cannot hope to take charge of a sophisticated capitalist society unless it can gain support from one of the major classes. Mass support from the working class is ruled out by the very nature of Nazism— even at their height the Nazis in Germany never polled more votes than the combined votes of the working class parties. In the unions the Nazis always polled less than 10 percent in shop steward elections. But support from the ruling class is possible—so long as the Nazis can offer them something that the traditional conservative parties cannot. Here we come to the distinctive feature of the Nazis' programme: the physical destruction of the workers' movement. This is what no normal conservative party offers—the street fighting force which can cow trade unionists and socialists through terror.

Some people find it hard to believe that the defining

characteristic of the Nazis is their organised attempt to smash the working class. Surely, they argue, racism is what the Nazis are about.

Certainly racism is often an important part of Nazi ideas, though not always. It played little role in Mussolini's fascist party, for instance, whose propaganda centred around 'smashing the reds'. Even in Germany, where the Nazis were hysterically anti Jewish, they did not get the crucial backing of big manufacturers, like Krupps and Thyssen because they wanted to exterminate the Jews, who in any case only made up a tiny percentage of the population. For the capitalists the power of the unions was the key problem, not 'the Jews'.

But racism suits the Nazis because it divides the working class and gives the Nazi stormtroopers a target which will not automatically, they hope, trigger mass resistance. Racism is the means, but crushing the working class is the aim, the only aim for which the ruling class is willing to back the Nazis.

On this understanding it is possible to build an effective strategy for opposing the Nazis.

The first step is to deny the Nazis the ability to build a street fighting organisation that can appeal to ruling class backers as a tool with which to break the workers' movement. To deny the Nazis this organisation means preventing them marching and organising on the streets—as anti-fascists did in Cable Street, east London, in 1936 or in Lewisham, south London, in 1977, or in Tower Hamlets a few years ago. These mobilisations were designed to act on the advice that Hitler himself once gave his opponents:

> *Only one thing could have stopped our movement—if our adversaries had understood its principle and, from the first day, had smashed with the utmost brutality the nucleus of our new movement.*

To do this effectively means mobilising everyone who is against the Nazis—black, Asian, immigrant and white, members of every trade union, Labour Party members and people who are in no political party as well as revolutionaries. But this united front has to be an activist organisation, not a talking shop, a consciousness raising group or a debating society. And it must restrict itself to mobilising the maximum numbers on the single issue of defeating the Nazis.

This is, of course, 'sticking-plaster politics', treating the symptom not the wider causes of racism or of economic discontent. But if you have been cut by a lunatic with a knife, a sticking-plaster is precisely what you need. Nevertheless if we are to avoid being cut again and again then we must also remove the lunacy which causes fascism. So within and alongside the united front against fascism we need to raise two issues.

Firstly, we need to insist that the battle against the closure of hospitals and schools, the destruction of the unions and worsening wages and conditions is vital not only in its own right, but also because it strikes at the roots of fascism. It replaces despair with faith in collective working class solutions to the crisis. In the battle to save every hospital we can insist that black, Asian, immigrant and white workers all built the NHS, all now run the NHS, and all use the NHS. For many this will be a convincing argument in favour of working class unity and against racism.

Secondly, we should argue that the threat of fascism will only finally be removed when the insane system that produces economic crises and social dislocation is replaced with a socialist society.

Agreement with these two arguments *are not pre-conditions* for joining the fight against the Nazis—if people don't agree with socialists on these, or any other, questions they are still more than welcome in the common fight against the fascists. But the more people that can be convinced of these arguments in the course of common struggle, the stronger the anti fascist movement will be and the nearer we will be to striking at the roots of fascism.

12. Immigration controls

The idea that Britain needs immigration controls finds support among workers who wouldn't touch the Nazis with a barge pole and who, in other circumstances, see themselves as anti racists. In recent years the rise of UKIP has given renewed life to the kind of prejudice that finds immigrants an easy target. One very important reason for this is that the Labour Party has always bowed to Tory racist arguments about immigration and has itself introduced many of the most barbaric immigration controls.

Merlyn Rees, then Labour's Home Secretary, admitted on TV in 1978 that immigration controls are not about 'stopping too many people coming into the country' but about stopping black people coming into the country. Rees was asked: 'What you really mean is that immigration control is a device to keep out coloured people?' He replied: 'That is what it is'. But since that time European Union immigration has given the prejudice a new face. 'We are not racists', the anti immigrant politicians say, 'we are against European white immigrants as much as black or Asian immigrants'.

But the truth is that immigrants have always come from all over the globe. Even before the European immigration of recent years there were more Europeans, New Zealanders and white South Africans coming to Britain than there are people from India, Bangladesh and Sri Lanka. Overall, only just over half the immigrants to this country were black or Asian.

In any case it has always been a lie to say that immigration must stop because 'Britain is full'. In reality Britain's population is growing very slowly. Official figures show that the UK population will only have risen by 15 percent by 2037—and only just over a quarter of that is from immigration.

And Britain's population is aging. The number of over 80s is set to double by 2037. Unless we have immigration the economy will shrivel, and with it the tax payments workers generate, and leave us all poorer.

Neither is it true that immigrants are taking jobs and houses from people born here. Only 200 thousand people came to Britain last year and yet there are, even on government figures, 2.3 million unemployed. Stopping immigration obviously won't solve the jobs crisis. Forcing the big corporations like the energy companies or the giant supermarket chains to spend some of their massive profits on providing jobs would, however, solve the problem. And if the Tory coalition government weren't refusing to build council houses there could be another 10,000 homes built every three weeks for people of every background.

In truth immigrants are not a drain on the economy. On the contrary, immigrants are educated and trained at somebody else's expense and they bring this to an economy short of skills. Most immigrants are young workers, whereas Britain has an ageing workforce. The cultural diversity immigrants provide is an enormous gain—Britain would be a much duller place without black, Asian and immigrant workers, writers, musicians and athletes. Its diet would certainly be worse without curries and kebabs, pasta and Chinese, Turkish, Vietnamese or Arabic food. If the racists would have us ban such diversity, where should we stop? With curries, or with the potato, imported from abroad over 400 years ago? With the mango, or with its fellow import, the tomato?

The capitalists, of course, recognise no borders. They, their money and even their factories are moved across continents in search of a profit. It is they who beckon immigrants here in times of boom, and then try to force them out or stop them coming during a slump. We have nothing to gain from playing their game. Workers are an international class. What unites us is far more important than our place of birth, our religion or the colour of our skin. Together we have the power to beat the bosses, but if we let them divide us they will exploit us all. That's why we want to scrap all immigration controls. Our message to all immigrants is: you're welcome here.

13. Why we are for women's liberation

Discrimination against women is not hard to see: when women are able to take full time jobs they are paid only two thirds of the average male wage; women still do far more housework and child care than men; women suffer sexual harassment and rape; and in everything from pornography to advertising women are portrayed as if their sexuality were the only important thing about them.

All women suffer this kind of oppression. Whether you are a princess or a pauper, women's oppression will touch your life—but not to the same degree.

There may still be fewer women company directors and fewer women MPs than there are male directors and MPs, but rich women can find ways of relieving the burden of oppression which simply are not available to working class women.

Housework and child care are hardly the same worry for working class women as for the women who can afford nursery provision, a nanny or a maid. Difficulties in getting an abortion can always be circumvented by women with enough money to go to private Harley Street clinics. It is poor women who will suffer even greater poverty because of unwanted children, or else face death and injury at the hands of the back street abortionist. A loveless relationship, perhaps involving domestic violence, is easier to escape if you have money. Rape and sexual harassment are easier to avoid if you can afford to run a car or hire a cab than if you have to walk or use public transport.

Indeed, rich women benefit from the oppression of poor women. The low wages paid to a Filipino maid or a working class child minder make a rich employer richer still. So women's oppression looks very different from the castle than from the cottage.

Political divisions based on class have always existed in the women's movement since its earliest days. For all that we celebrate the suffragette movement's achievements, it divided over the importance of organising working class women. Sylvia Pankhurst became a supporter of the Bolshevik revolution, organising women in London's East End. Christabel and Emmeline Pankhurst courted the middle class and became right wingers and supporters of the First World War.

Similarly, the women's movement of the 1960s and 1970s divided over class issues—some have became or remained socialists but many others have found cosy niches in middle class professions. To see why this happens we need to understand why women are oppressed. The answer lies in the way capitalism works.

Capitalists need two things in order to make a profit. They need factories and machines, offices and banks. But they also need a healthy and educated workforce—and that costs money. The state provides some of what is needed for such a workforce, like the NHS and the education system, although the money still comes mostly from taxes on the working class. But a great deal the of time, effort and money that is needed to reproduce a new workforce each generation comes from the private family.

This is the key to women's oppression: the system largely depends on women's unpaid labour in the home for the creation of a fit and educated workforce. Everything else about women's oppression—the lower paid jobs, the sexual stereotyping and the physical attacks—bolsters women's role in housework and child care.

Two conclusions follow. Firstly, it is the way in which capitalism works that creates the institutions and values which lead to the oppression of women, not the interests of men, either individually or as a group. The interests that different men have in maintaining women's oppression are diametrically opposed depending on whether they are from the ruling class or the working class.

Working class men gain nothing if women are paid low wages or excluded from the workforce. The bosses use low paid women workers as a lever to lower the wages of all workers. The more equal and the higher women's wages, the more women have access to full employment, the better the chances of all workers' wages and job prospects rising. Equally, working class men do not benefit from their partners being driven to exhaustion by the double burden of child care and a job. Male and female workers have an interest in better, free nurseries, cheap laundries and restaurant facilities.

Ruling class men, on the contrary, have every interest in keeping women in the home to provide cheap domestic labour and in keeping them as second class workers, perpetuating divisions in the working class and dragging down the pay and conditions of all workers. Many ruling class women, whose wealth depends on the exploitation of workers, will therefore also support the continued oppression of women, even if they might campaign for their own equality within the establishment.

Secondly, it follows that the strategy of some feminists of uniting all women against all men is fatally flawed. Many working class men can be won to supporting demands for women's liberation, while many ruling class and middle class women cannot.

Socialists are for women's liberation in all and every instance. We are even for reforms that seem to mainly benefit middle class women. But for liberation to mean anything to the vast majority of working class women, and for it to be successful, it must be part of a wider class struggle. If, in reaction to the experience of oppression women choose to organise separately, socialists will defend their right to do so. But we do not see such separation from working class men as the most effective way to challenge oppression—for that the maximum amount of class unity is necessary.

We do not expect women to be the only ones fighting for liberation, anymore than we expect only the victims of racism to struggle to end it. Women will often take the lead, of course, but it is the task of every socialist, and every trade unionist to fight for women's liberation. However, even in the day to day battles against the effects of the oppression of women, a class analysis and a separatist feminist analysis will suggest quite different strategies. The first will look to the trade union and labour movement, seeking to fight to gain its support for women's demands. The second will look to middle class women, separatist organisation and, often, despite radical rhetoric, Labour Party or NGO-inspired lobbying.

Socialists should aim to unite our class in struggle, not to tie its hands with separate organisation or by allowing the middle classes to limit its horizons and methods.

14. Why we are for LGBT liberation

Right-wing politicians and media commentators are always trying to find a scapegoat to blame for the failings of their system. Single parents, black people, and travellers have all been blamed for the social decay we see all around us. Gays and lesbians—or indeed anyone who's sexual choices fall outside the mainstream—are another favourite scapegoat. Just as socialists defend these other oppressed groups, we should oppose oppression based on sexual orientation.

The oppression of those with 'non-mainstream' sexual orientation is closely linked with capitalism's need to reproduce new generations of workers at minimum cost. The best way for the system to achieve this is to push as much as possible of the cost of child care and housework onto working class individuals themselves. This is why the establishment promotes the idea that the only 'normal' way to live is in the 'married with two kids' family set up.

Yet most households today are not made up of 'normal' families. Single people, unmarried couples with no children, houses with more than one family living in them, or single parents are now in the majority.

But it doesn't seem to matter how far reality diverges from the traditional picture, we are still bombarded with images of the stereotypical family. Food comes in 'family packs' (why not just 'large size'?), politicians preach 'family values' (as if married people are the only values' (as if people in 'normal' famileis are only ones who love their kids or care for their partners), while the church frowns on unmarried couples (despite the fact that one in three marriages end in divorce and surveys show that unmarried couples are happier).

Everyone suffers under this socially enforced regime because they are obliged to live in a pattern much more rigid than they want their lives to be. This 'order' is imposed on our personal, emotional and sexual lives to suit the needs of the system, not to suit our own needs. To live outside this 'order' is to suffer discrimination because your sexual preference doesn't fit the imposed pattern. Lesbians and gays and others with a different sexual orientation appear as a standing affront to the moralists and bigots. They seem to live lives utterly at odds with family values and they obviously have sex 'purely for pleasure, not to procreate'! As a result lesbians and gays can often find themselves sacked or refused a job because of their sexuality, constantly pilloried in the press, discriminated against in the housing market and subjected to verbal and physical assault. They may be denied the right to adopt or to artificial insemination because of their sexuality.

It should always be a matter of principle for socialists to oppose such oppression.

The resistance to such oppression from gays and lesbians themselves grew enormously in the late 1960s. The great civil rights struggle by American black people, the massive resistance to the Vietnam War, the general strike in France, the international student struggles and the birth of the modem women's movement all had their effect on gays and lesbians.

This was the era when the Gay Liberation Front was born, taking its name from the Vietnamese National Liberation Front. It was the birth of organised, political resistance by gays and lesbians. The resistance looked to other oppressed groups and to the socialist movement for solidarity. But there was always a division at the heart of the gay movement because their oppression, like that of women, touches people from every class but does not touch them equally.

Those who can afford not to travel on public transport, to avoid poor housing and to be part of the growing pink economy of clubs and pubs, can often shield themselves from the worst oppression. A working class person, perhaps living at home or with little contact with other gays or lesbians does not have the same opportunities.

This is why a higher proportion of middle class than working class gays and lesbians come out openly about their sexuality. It is also why some gays and lesbians believe that their oppression can be beaten by changing their personal lifestyle—lifestyle politics. It can seem as if establishing a comfortable way of life where discrimination is partially held at bay and LGBT identity celebrated is all that can be achieved.

However understandable, this can only ever be a partial answer and may ultimately be a self defeating strategy. It can lead away from unity with the working class movement and other oppressed groups because it stresses what separates gays and lesbians from others, not what all the oppressed and exploited have in common.

Socialists argue the best way to fight for gay and lesbian liberation lies in fighting for unity in the working class movement. It hasn't always easy to convince people to support gays and lesbians, though it is a lot easier today because of such efforts in the past. But such unity is possible because all workers, gay and straight, face the same enemy. The system which denies gays an equal age of consent also denies all workers a decent wage. The police victimise gays *and* protestors.

Here, in the common class interest that most gays and lesbians share with all workers, is the key to liberation. A gay movement which cuts itself off from such allies may form a vocal minority and will always get support from socialists. It is nevertheless throwing away the very weapon that our common enemy fears most—a politically conscious, united working class movement.

15. Liberation and socialist revolution

Women, black people, gays and lesbians are oppressed groups in capitalist society. Socialists support all their struggles against discrimination, even campaigns for more women and black people to become company directors or MPs, or for women and black police officers to be free of harassment and discrimination within the force. If, in reaction to the experience of oppression, women or gays and lesbians choose to organise separately we will defend their right to do so, especially when they are under attack from the media or the right wing in the labour movement.

But we do not think that either the fight to be treated equally within the establishment, or separation from the working class movement is the most effective way to fight oppression. Both strategies leave untouched the oppression of most working class women, black people, gays and lesbians.

The most effective forms of protest, like the successive campaigns that won abortion rights in this country, have involved both men and women, black and white, and have increasingly looked to the trade union movement for practical and financial solidarity. When it comes to a fundamental transformation of society to rid us of oppression, not merely reform its worst manifestations, the root cause of oppression has to be addressed. This lies in the capitalist system's need for cheap labour, in its need to force the costs of reproducing the workforce onto the private family and the sexual stereotypes this creates.

So it is that those who are oppressed because they are women or because of their sexuality face the same enemy as those who are exploited and oppressed because they are workers—the capitalist class. Of course the media and the establishment politicians do their best to hide this common interest shared by workers and the oppressed. Capitalism has always sought to set different groups of the oppressed and exploited against each other.

But in the course of the struggle it is possible to convince workers—men and women, whatever their sexual orientation, race or religion—that liberation is only possible by undermining capitalism as a whole. This requires a united working class movement which supports the struggles of the oppressed and is therefore capable of winning them to carrying through a revolution. That is why there can be no liberation of the oppressed without socialism and no socialism without the liberation of the oppressed.

16. Class solidarity and national liberation

Socialists think of the world as divided into classes.

The working class is an international class, found everywhere from Maryland to Moscow. So too is the capitalist class whose huge multinational firms now stretch across the globe. Economic integration is ensuring that the world's workers increasingly wear similar clothes, watch the same TV programmes and work for the same employers.

But at the same time as the world is being drawn together, economically it is also being divided by nation states. Each little patch of earth has its own government and laws, flags and anthems, border guards and barbed wire, immigration controls and labour laws.

If all nations were equal, if their economies were of equal size and their armed forces of equal strength, internationalism would be easy. All socialists would have to do is call for workers to unite across the boundaries of nation states in common struggle against the international ruling class. In many instances, this is exactly the right thing to do. When German metal workers, American miners or Australian dockers go on strike socialists argue for international solidarity strikes, boycotts, collections and messages of support.

But because nations are not all equal, there are many cases where things are not so straightforward. Capitalism has developed unevenly, first in Europe and America and then progressively in every corner of the world. The first capitalist powers used their new found strength to build empires. They used their industrial and financial strength, and the armies and navies which that strength allowed them to build, to invade, subdue and colonise other, less economically developed countries. The empire building countries drained great wealth from the countries they invaded, further limiting the colonised nations' economic development. The British, Spanish, Dutch, French, German, American, Russian, Japanese and Italian rulers—to name only the most powerful—carved out colonies and dependencies in India, Asia, Ireland, the Far East, the Middle East, Africa, the Caribbean and Latin America.

Today, although the formal colonies have largely gone, the major powers still dominate the weaker ones. Unless the smaller powers do as they are told bank loans are withheld, foreign aid refused, tariff walls erected, diplomatic cooperation denied or trade embargoes imposed. If all this fails, the major powers use the overwhelming military force at their disposal to get their own way. The major powers have an impressive array of institutions to impose their will on poorer countries: economic power is wielded through the World Bank, the International Monetary Fund and the European Union. Diplomatic and military pressure can be added by the United Nations and NATO. This is the system of imperialism.

Small countries and oppressed nationalities have, not surprisingly, revolted against this imperialist order. From the centuries of fighting for Irish independence through the right for Indian independence to the struggles of Iraqi or Afghan people against military occupation, the imperialist powers have always faced resistance.

These struggles are not usually working class struggles for socialism They are struggles for national liberation, struggles to allow the indigenous people to govern themselves. Today, they are often struggles by people who have already achieved their own nation state to prevent the major powers from interfering in the policy of that state. Although workers are often involved in such struggles, they are not usually led by workers but by middle class or establishment politicians supported by at least some elements of the ruling class. This, for instance, was the case in Saddam Hussein's Iraq during the Gulf War.

What should socialists say in such circumstances? Many are tempted to say 'a plague on both your houses'. They do not like what the imperialist powers are doing, but they don't see why they should support people who just want to carve out their own little nation as a minor version of what the big powers have already got, especially if the leader of the poorer nation is a tyrant.

But there is a serious flaw in the 'plague on both your houses' attitude. Both houses are not equal. On the one side there are the most powerful armed forces in the world, backed up by the most powerful economies in the world. On the other, there are poor countries being kept poor by the rich nations. Their natural resources, like oil in the Middle East, are plundered and their finances are crippled by repayments to Western banks. In conflicts between such countries, say between America and Cuba, we are not looking at a fight between two equal powers, like Germany and Britain in the First World War. We are looking at a powerful oppressor and a much weaker, oppressed nation.

Socialists should unconditionally stand with the oppressed nation against the oppressor nation, even if the people who run the oppressed country are undemocratic and persecute minorities, as Saddam Hussein persecuted Kurds and Castro persecuted gay people.

If the imperialist powers, like Britain and America, win such conflicts then the whole imperialist system will be strengthened and with it the power of the ruling classes in the imperialist countries over their own working class. But if the oppressed countries defeat the imperialist powers, as the Vietnamese defeated the Americans in the 1970s, then the whole imperialist system and the domestic position of the ruling class in the great powers is weakened. This is precisely what happened to the American ruling class after Vietnam. This is why the left internationally were right to call for victory to the Vietnamese National Liberation Front, despite the fact that many had very profound political differences with the NLF.

So should socialists just keep quiet about their political differences with those who lead national liberation struggles? Should we, for instance, simply not mention the fact that we fundamentally disagree with the social conservatism of the Taliban or that we do not share the politics of Hamas in Palestine?

No, we should be clear that we believe the Taliban are behaving in ways that undermine their own support and make it more difficult to defeat imperialism. We can be clear that we do not think that Hamas always fights in the most effective way. We must encourage the building of left and progressive forces in Afghanistan and Palestine which are also anti-imperialist, while rejecting those who criticise the Taliban or Hamas but are effectively pro-imperialist. The same perspective applies elsewhere since national liberation movements, by definition, try to unite bosses and workers to fight imperialism.

But we do not make it a condition of our being opposed to imperialism that any force also fighting imperialism—be that the IRA, Hamas, or the Taliban—accept such criticism or join our organisation. Even if they reject our criticism, we would still rather side with the oppressed than with one of the most powerful imperialist countries in the world. Our support is, therefore, critical but unconditional.

This way we hope to both side with the oppressed nations against the imperialist nations and, at the same time, develop a socialist opposition within the oppressed nations to fight both the imperialists and the ruling class, or would-be ruling class, of their own nation.

This means combining the class struggle with the struggle against imperialism, turning the struggle for national liberation into a struggle for socialism.

For our part, socialists in the imperialist countries can ensure that by struggling against imperialism we do not allow our own ruling class to set black worker against white worker or to get us to accept lower wages or worse conditions by calls to 'support our country' or, in times of armed conflict, 'make sacrifices for the war'. To support the struggle of poorer countries is, simultaneously, to fight against the growth of nationalistic and racist ideas in our own ranks and, therefore, a struggle for working class unity. It is not an act of charity but an act of self defence.

17. Socialism and state ownership

There has always been a widespread feeling on the left that nationalisation or state ownership is inevitably a socialist measure. Labour Party supporters often argue this as proof that working within the system can deliver reforms that will lead to socialism. For many years people who believed that the Stalinist regimes in Eastern Europe were socialist pointed to state control of the economy as proof of their case. In the Third World many leaders of national liberation struggles argued that state ownership meant that former colonies were on the road to socialism.

All three of these strands of thought are now in full scale retreat before the gale of free market 'liberalisation' which has been blowing through the world since the 1980s. Labour Party leaders never now talk of nationalisation. The states of Eastern Europe are now ruled by pro-marketeers, though they are often yesterday's state bureaucrats newly dressed in City suits. And in the poor countries visions of state-led economic development have wilted under the twin blows of recession and debt repayment.

Yet ideology is in fact running ahead of reality. The state is still a vital economic force in all these societies. But is it a force for socialism?

A moment's thought tells us that nationalisation cannot be an inherently socialist measure. Hitler's Nazi state was, after all, one of the biggest nationalisers of the twentieth century. The Japanese post war economic miracle was achieved by very close state direction of the economy. And the third biggest economy in the world is the one composed of the United States Atomic Energy Authority, the space agency NASA and the Pentagon~a massive state owned trust thundering away in the heart of 'free market' America. Not even the most devout advocate of state ownership would claim that these societies are anything but capitalist.

The crucial point here is to ask the right question. Instead of asking, 'Does the state own industry?' socialists should ask, 'Who controls the state?' Where workers have not taken control of society, where the capitalists still control the state, nationalisation simply produces state capitalism, not socialism.

Frederick Engels made the same point over 100 years ago in his *Socialism, Utopian and Scientific*:

> *The modern state, whatever its form, is essentially a capitalist machine, the state of the capitalists, the ideal aggregate capitalist. The more productive forces it takes over into its possession, the more it becomes a real aggregate capitalist the more citizens it exploits. The workers remain wage workers, proletarians. The capitalist relationship is not abolished, rather it is pushed to its limit.*

Engels goes on to joke that if state ownership alone were enough to define something as socialist then 'the Royal Maritime Company, the Royal Porcelain Manufacture, and even the regimental tailors in the army would be socialist institutions'.

But surely, some argue, it is different when whole economies, like those which existed in Eastern Europe, are taken over by people who call themselves socialists? Surely when national liberation movements, as in Castro's Cuba, take over a society they can move towards .socialism in a way that partial nationalisation in a capitalist economy cannot?

This would be true enough—if the working class had

taken power in Eastern Europe or Cuba. But they did not. There were no workers' revolutions in Eastern Europe in 1945, no elected workers' councils, no elected factory committees, no workers' militia. It was the Russian army, not the working class, which put the 'communist' leaders in power. Those leaders controlled industry by appointing bosses every bit as unaccountable and exploitative as their Western counterparts.

Cuba, like many other Third World 'socialist' regimes, is different. Here there was an uprising against US imperialism, and every socialist supported it. The Cuban people had every right to chuck out the corrupt, brutal, US backed Batista dictatorship. They still have every right to fight the US blockade and the US inspired diplomatic and military pressure which is trying to wreck their society. But all this should not lead us to conclude that Cuba and similar regimes are socialist. The popular rising which overthrew Batista hardly involved the working class, though it initially had the sympathy of many workers. The revolt followed a classic pattern for Third World liberation struggles. It was led by middle class exiles who returned to begin a guerrilla war, supported by the peasantry and conducted from the countryside.

Once in power Castro, like the leaders of the Eastern bloc, would have been happy to trade with market economies. The Cold War blockade put paid to that option in both cases. State ownership was the alternative.

But state ownership without workers' control does not free a society from the grip of capitalism. Both the Third World regimes and the Eastern European states still had to compete with the West for international markets. They had to borrow from Western banks. And, more importantly, they had to match the West militarily, tank for tank, missile for missile. Such international pressure determined the domestic relationship between the state and the working class. If Western workers were forced to work harder, then the state capitalist regimes had to force

their workers to work harder. If armaments manufacturers in the West increased productivity, then so must the
state owned arms manufacturers elsewhere. The states in
Eastern Europe performed and those in the Third World
perform all the same functions that the capitalist class
and its states do in Western societies.

Only when workers democratically control society
will we have socialism. Socialism cannot be built unless
workers control the factories and the political institutions.

This does not mean, however, that there are not
important occasions where socialists should support
nationalisation. But we should judge it using the same
yardstick that we use when we ask 'is a society socialist or
not?' We should ask 'does this increase the confidence of
workers, their living standards and their ability to organise, or not?' So the formation of the NHS in Britain did,
of course, have the support of all socialists. The privatisation and subsequent closure of the coal industry, with its
massive job losses, was opposed by every socialist. Every
socialist defends the NHS from privatisation. We all want
the rail and energy companies taken into public ownership. We'd all be better off if the banks were nationalised.

If socialists keep these criteria in mind—are workers
directly in control of their own lives and have they won
these gains by their own struggles, do they benefit from
nationalisation?—we will not only be able to distinguish
between genuine socialism and state capitalism, we will
also be able to give solidarity to struggles for national liberation in the Third World without believing that they are
necessarily going to lead to socialism. Such criteria will
also enable us to distinguish within such Third World
conflicts those workers' struggles which can carry workers beyond national liberation towards international
revolution and the creation of a socialist society.

18. What is a socialist revolution?

The capitalist state is, in the words of Marx and Engels, 'a mechanism for forcibly holding down the exploited class in conditions of oppression' and that is why 'the working class cannot simply lay hold of the ready made state machinery and wield it for its own purposes'.

That is one reason why a revolution is necessary. It has to clear away the old state and replace it with a workers' state. But what would a workers' state be like? Where would it come from?

Luckily, history provides us with some ideas. In past struggles we can find attempts to set up workers' states. These attempts usually started from organisations built to fight the old order and then, when the old order was shaken, these same bodies organised its overthrow. After the revolution these organisations grew still further to take on the tasks of running society. So a revolution isn't just a bolt from the blue. A revolution is much more than the moment of insurrection, it is also a process.

Look at what happened during the Russian revolution of 1905. A strike committee started by organising against print employers, ignited more general resistance and became a workers' council involving all the different sections of the working class. It then challenged the government for the power to run society.

The Paris Commune of 1871 was a similar attempt to set up a workers' state. Marx left this description of how it worked:

The Commune was formed of the municipal councillors, chosen by universal suffrage in the various wards of Paris, responsible and revocable at any time. The majority of its members were naturally working men, or the acknowledged representatives of the working class... The police, which until then had been the instrument of the government, was at once stripped of its political attributes, and turned into the responsible and at all times revocable instrument of the Commune... From the members of the Commune downwards, public service had to be done at workmen's wages. The privileges and the representation allowances of the high dignitaries of state disappeared along with the dignitaries themselves... Having once got rid of the standing army and the police, the instruments of the physical force of the old government, the Commune proceeded at once to break the instrument of spiritual suppression, the power of the priests... The judicial functionaries lost their sham independence... they were thenceforward to be elective, responsible and revocable.

The workers' councils which emerged again in Russia in 1917 were an even more advanced form of working class self organisation. But the essence was the same~complete democracy in all areas of life, the removal of special pay and status for representatives, all representatives, from judges to militia officers, to be recalled instantly if they did not carry out the wishes of those who voted for them.

This is very different from the capitalist state. Instead of an instrument wielded by a tiny rich minority to hold down the majority, it is the democratic organisation of the majority designed to prevent the old ruling class regaining its power. But as soon as the threat of counter revolution is beaten back and the power of the old ruling class broken even this, the most democratic state in history, will be unnecessary. Engels writes:

As soon as there is no longer a class to be held in subjection any longer, as soon as class domination and the struggle for individual existence based

*on anarchy of production existing up to now are
eliminated... there is nothing left to repress, nothing necessitating a special repressive force, a state...
The interference of the state power in social relations
becomes superfluous in one sphere after another, and
then it dies away of itself... The state is not abolished,
it withers away.*

A socialist revolution will also start the process of
transforming the economy. Capitalism glories in the
idea of a 'free market'. Firms produce what they want,
when they want. Their only aim is to make a profit. If that
means that a profit can be made out of giant fluffy dice
to hang from the rear-view mirror of a car, rather than
from food for the starving, then fluffy dice it is. Nuclear
weapons or more schools? It depends on what makes a
profit. But even when capitalists think they've got a profit
making item, they can't be sure. Perhaps six other firms
have all had the same idea. So to add to the waste of producing fluffy dice, we may well end up with fluffy dice
that no one will buy. Once that happens jobs will be lost
and then people will have even less money to spend.

To overcome this chaos, production needs to be
planned. The idea of planning is very unfashionable
these days. People think it has to mean the grey uniform-
ity of the old Stalinist states. But they were a parody of
planning. Workers had no control over production and
distribution, yet this is the first requirement of socialist
planning.

Some people go on to argue that planning is impossible because the economy is far too complex. They forget
that great big chunks of the economy are already very
closely planned.

Consider what happens when your food packages
are run over the bar code reader at the supermarket. A
message is sent to the stockroom computer to show how
fast stocks are declining. This information is sent on to

the warehouse so replacement stocks can be sent. The warehouse stock figures are aggregated by head office so that they can inform their wholesale suppliers. The wholesalers plan how much they want from farmers and importers. The whole process, from the farmer's field to the supermarket shelf, is a series of planned decisions. It is ready made for the kind of planning that a socialist society would need. It doesn't work under capitalism because there isn't any co-ordinated overall planning. Tesco has a plan—but so does Sainsburys, Asda, Morrisons, and Lidl—all designed to wreck each other's markets.

Neither would replacing these competing plans with one plan reduce diversity and choice—after all, virtually the same goods are on sale in all these supermarkets. Indeed the choice of products could be significantly increased just by using resources that are now squandered by useless duplication across all the supermarket chains. And in the choice of which brand of, say, chocolate biscuit to produce price signals, as economists call the spending decisions we take, might well have a role. Socialists don't want to, even if we could, plan all the details of consumer purchase.

But what we could do is to vote on how our large scale spending priorities are to be ordered. Would we vote for more hospitals or more weapons? More houses or more schools? They won't always be easy choices. There will be a lot of debate. But they will be our choices not the imposed priorities of a market made for profit. By doing away with the waste and exploitation of capitalism we will have given ourselves far more resources than we can possibly imagine having in this society.

19. Can workers run society?

One of the age-old objections to socialism is that workers are incapable of running society. 'People have to have someone to tell them what to do,' goes the time worn refrain. One look at the way our society actually runs, as opposed to the way the bosses and the media tell us it runs, shows that nothing could be further from the truth.

The myth is that if it weren't for bosses and managers everything would grind to a halt~yet many a factory occupation or work-in has proved the opposite. When shipbuilders and motorbike manufacturing workers occupied their factories in the 1970s the quality of the goods actually improved. Workers know their jobs, and collectively they know the whole production process, better than any manager—which is why firms make millions of pounds a year implementing ideas given to them in suggestion boxes on production lines and why 'Japanese' quality control circles try to tap the initiative and knowledge of workers to increase product quality.

In any case, many managers, supervisors and foremen were workers themselves before they were promoted. More often than not any specialised knowledge about how things are produced was acquired while they were workers, not after they became managers. Usually what makes such people suitable managers is their willingness to sack people, cut wages and generally boss people around. This, and not anything useful, is certainly what they are taught on management training courses.

By contrast, there is no factory or office in the world that can run if the workers stop work. No management group has ever produced a car, collected the rubbish or run a bus service if workers refuse to do their job.

Some people will agree to all this, but then object that,

even though workers may be able to run their own local workplace very well without the boss, they couldn't manage the more complex task of making the whole society work. How could workers decide whether we should build roads or railways, coordinate health care and education, or decide between the production of food and luxury goods? Surely, the argument goes, the bosses are necessary for these big decisions?

Strangely enough, bosses and managers don't really decide these things even now. How do we know? Because they are always telling us that they don't. When a car factory is closed, ministers and managers are the first to say that they aren't responsible—it's 'the market' that decides. If there is chaos on the roads and public transport is falling to pieces, the government tells us this is because people choose to buy cars and not to pay the fares on public transport—the market has decided.

In a sense, the bosses and the ministers are, for once, telling the truth. They are the servants of the market. Of course they always make sure that they are the last to be damaged if the market turns against them. It is always our wages, jobs or conditions that go first—and their job is to make sure it stays that way. But once the system of market competition and profit making is up and running everyone in the system has to live by its rules. That's why 'workers co-ops' can only ever be short lived. Competition from more ruthless wage cutting firms meant that, even though the workers in this or that firm were perfectly capable of running the local plant, they would have to behave like bosses if they wanted to continue the struggle with their more ruthless competitors.

That's why if workers want to be able to run society they have to take it over all at once, not just one factory or office at a time. Only by taking over the whole society can workers control the relations between the different firms as well as the set-up inside the firm. If we don't take over the whole thing then the competition between the firms forces us to behave like bosses inside the firm—that's why the miners who took over Monktonhall colliery in Scotland after the Great Miners' Strike ended up paying worse wages and employing fewer miners than British Coal had.

If we did take the whole society over, would there be a better way of organising things than the market? Many people would be tempted to say that we could hardly do worse than the market. We wouldn't let millions rot on the dole, spend billions on nuclear weapons while the health and education systems crumble, or waste billions more on advertising while a quarter of people in Britain live below the poverty line. These kind of priorities are set by a ruling class whose only concerns are profit and having a big enough army, police and prison system to defend their profits. Our priorities would be decided democratically. We would meet together in workers' councils and vote on economic priorities, just as we now elect shop stewards and union officers, after debate and discussion.

Because we would control the factories, offices, hospitals and schools we would see that our decisions got carried out. We would implement what we had decided. That's why workers' power would be so different from a Labour government where all the good promises are broken because the rich who own the newspapers, control the economy and run Whitehall sabotage them.

When we decide what to produce and implement the decisions, when everyone can see what is happening in every part of the society, then all the pent up energies, unused skills and cramped imagination of workers can be set free on the collective task of building a society without exploitation, oppression and the rule of the tiny few.

20. What happened in Russia?

In October 1917 the Russian working class became the first exploited class in history to hold power for more than a few weeks. Workers took control of the factories, offices, transport facilities, banks and government offices. Peasants seized the land they had tilled for generations and expelled the landlords who had dominated their lives from the time before Russia was even a nation.

The Council (or Soviet, to use the Russian word) of Workers', Soldiers' and Peasants' Deputies became the first government to stop a war simply by refusing to fight any longer, beginning the process that ended the First World War. The racism which had, under the old regime, resulted in the mass murder of Jews was now confined to the territories where the counter revolution still held sway. The revolution recognised Leon Trotsky, a Jew, as its leader.

For the first time a woman became a government minister. Divorce and abortion were available on demand. And for the first time laws discriminating against gay people were abolished. New and exciting forms of art flourished, not just in the galleries, but in the streets and factories. The revolution was, as Lenin had predicted, 'a festival of the oppressed'.

But the Russian Revolution contained a fatal weakness. It did not take place in an industrialised country where the working class were the majority.

This mattered because socialism needs an economy capable of generating a reasonable amount of goods and services if it is to work. Slaves in ancient Rome or medieval peasants couldn't make a socialist revolution—the societies in which they lived just weren't rich enough to guarantee all the poor a secure and prosperous life.

Capitalism is different. The productivity of workers in modem industrialised society is great enough to ensure, if they make a revolution, they inherit an economy powerful enough to underpin an egalitarian society.

While this is true generally, true of capitalism as an international system, it is not necessarily true of every country taken in isolation. This doesn't mean that a revolution can't start in a poor country. But it does mean that it can't be completed in a poor country. For it to survive it must spread to richer countries with bigger working classes and stronger economies.

This idea of spreading the revolution informed the whole strategy pursued by its leaders, Lenin and Trotsky. They reasoned that Russia was tied to other countries by the international market, by financial links, by Western investment in Russia and by common participation in the First World War. If Russia started a revolution, they argued, other countries would not be far behind.

They were right. Finland, Germany, Hungary and Bulgaria all had revolutions in the aftermath of 1917. But they were ultimately all defeated, largely because none were led by a party like Lenin and Trotsky's Bolsheviks.

Consequently, the Russian Revolution was thrown back on its own inadequate resources at a time when every major imperialist power, plus some others, were trying to crush the revolution by force. So it was that between 1918 and 1922 a working class of just 3 million out of a total population of 160 million, racked by famine and strangled by an international blockade, faced 14 invading armies and domestic counter revolution from the old ruling class. The Russian Revolution was cornered and fighting for its life. The Red Army was scraped together from nothing. Even forced grain requisitioning couldn't prevent starvation. Industry, already in a parlous state after the war, virtually disintegrated.

The working class was decimated. Many died fighting the counter revolution. Many more deserted the famine and disease ridden cities to return to family farms. By the end of the civil war the revolution had survived, but the working class had not. 'The working class has ceased to exist,' declared Lenin.

You can have many things without a working class, but a workers' state is not one of them. The class that had thronged through the hallways of the workers' councils, that had held mass meetings in every workplace, that struck and struggled for the revolution was atomised, leaving the state that it had created suspended in mid-air. Without the struggle, without the hectic debate which the struggle created, the state became less and less democratic, more and more bureaucratic.

After Lenin's death in 1924 those, like Trotsky, who wanted to return to the democratic traditions of the revolution found themselves increasingly isolated. In previous battles Lenin and Trotsky had always been able to rely on the self activity of the working class. That was no longer an option. Trotsky was forced to fight the rising bureaucracy, headed by Stalin, on the bureaucracy's terms. And with each new defeat on the international front—like the missed revolutionary opportunities in Germany in 1923 and China in 1927—Stalin's power became greater and Trotsky's chances of success diminished.

Stalin developed the theory of Socialism in One Country~the complete opposite of Lenin and Trotsky's internationalism. In reality, Socialism in One Country meant industrial development to catch up with the advanced countries, which in turn meant exploiting workers as hard as other countries, not spreading revolution. Competition between Stalin's state and other industrialised countries ensured that the state would exploit the Russian working class, just as competition between different capitalist firms obliges each capitalist to exploit the workers in his or her factory.

As Stalin used the state to re-introduce the old

exploitation all the old oppressions returned as well. Peasants were driven from the land onto collectivised farms. Racism and national chauvinism returned. The oppression of women returned, new art was suppressed.

To do all this Stalin had to crush every last remnant of the revolutionary tradition, especially the old Bolshevik Party. Lenin's 'testament', which called for Stalin's removal as general secretary of the party, was suppressed after Lenin's death. The vast majority of the Lenin's central committee, and many other party members, were killed in the great purges of the 1930s. Trotsky was killed by Stalin's agent in 1940. By then Stalin had long established a state capitalist society on the ruins of the Russian Revolution. Stalin's state performed all the same functions jointly performed by the capitalists and their states in the West.

Today, the state capitalist regime in Russia, and those modelled on it in Eastern Europe, lie in ruins. They were broken by revolt from below and pressure from the international market with which they tried to compete. But for East European workers the main battle lies ahead. They are still ruled by a tiny elite of super rich. Poverty still haunts them. Racism is still rife. The market has failed.

Workers everywhere can draw an important lesson from this spectacle: neither state capitalism nor market capitalism are capable of meeting their most elementary needs. Only when workers once again run society, as they did in the early years of the Russian Revolution, will we be able to do away with poverty and unemployment, racism and homelessness, the oppression of women and decaying welfare services.

Today, the working class in nearly every country is bigger than the Russian working class of 1917. The prospects for international revolution are better than at any time in human history.

21. Why we need a revolutionary organisation

If the Tory dream were to suddenly come true and every worker went along with pro-capitalist ideas, if there were never any strikes or protests, if no one ever answered back to the boss, then there would be no point in organising a socialist party.

We would be living in the kind of world George Orwell described in 1984: a cowed and submissive working class, afraid even to think a subversive thought, constantly monitored by Big Brother. In such a world the possibility of resistance, let alone revolution, would be reduced to nothing. Similarly, there would be no need for a socialist party if the anarchist dream of spontaneous class struggle came true. If, without organisation, planning or strategy, workers across the face of industry were suddenly to take action, there would be no need for socialist organisation.

But real life is never as bad as the Tory dream and never as good as the anarchist dream. In reality, working class struggle is always uneven, never uniformly bad or uniformly good. Some factories, offices or industries strike while others remain at work. Some within a workplace will vote for a strike, while others will not. Some will protest and demonstrate while others stay at home. Some workers are revolutionary socialists, some good militants, while others are Tories or scabs.

Most of the time revolutionary socialists will be a minority, and so are hardline Tories or anti union figures. Most workers, most of the time, will believe in a mixture of ideas. They could be pro-union, but still vote Tory. Perhaps they will want to strike, but worry about breaking the anti union laws. Maybe they will be against the Nazis, but still believe in the need for immigration controls. On any given issue they may be swayed by the right wing elements in the union or workplace, or they may be convinced by the arguments of the socialists.

A revolutionary socialist organisation groups together the workers who want to fight so that they can have the maximum chance of winning the majority of their fellow workers to taking action.

To stand the best chance of doing this, the militant minority will need to be clear and confident about their arguments and their strategy. They will need to know what is happening in other parts of the country where their tactics have already proved successful or where those of the right wing have already led to failure. They will need to back up their arguments with leaflets and with a newspaper that reports their actions and discussions.

They will want to know their enemy—what the government and the bosses are planning, what the employers' strategy is, whether they are divided among themselves or not. They will want to know what the leaders on our side are up to and how to counter any arguments designed to delay the struggle. They will want to connect their struggles with others who are fighting and from whom they may be able to get solidarity. They will need to know about the international experience of workers' struggles and about the history of the workers' movement—about what led to victory and what led to defeat in the past.

All this requires socialist organisation. It requires meetings for education and discussion, to hammer out tactics and to organise solidarity. It requires a website, regular printed material and other publications that report and analyse the struggle, which provide ideas and theory. It requires active organisation to bring all this experience to bear on the class struggle. It means organising to unite our class's struggles, just as the Tories, the employers and the government unite their class in struggle. In short, it requires a socialist party.

Such an organisation cannot reflect the average consciousness in the class~that would simply reproduce the confusions of those who are caught between Tory ideas and socialist ideas. You can't win an argument with someone if you are as confused as they are. Only if there is a network composed of those who are already clear about their strategy can it hope to present a forceful enough case to win others who, at first, only half agree with it

Some parties, of course, are deliberately designed to reproduce the contradictory mixture of ideas that many workers hold. The Labour Party purposely tries to mirror this confusion because it is not interested in raising workers' consciousness and willingness to fight. It is interested merely in winning elections. For winning elections blurring the issues, fudging, and reflecting people's half formed ideas is an attractive, though not always successful, strategy. An organisation designed to promote action cannot suffer such confusion. It must agree its principles and go out and argue for them even if, at first it is a minority.

But if a socialist organisation shouldn't dissolve itself into the rest of the class, it shouldn't stand aloof from the class either. It has to be involved in the struggle wherever workers or the oppressed are fighting back. It shouldn't preach or assume that it knows all the answers.

It should try to give a lead, but it should also listen. Lenin and the Bolsheviks didn't invent the idea of a workers' council, Russian workers did that themselves in the 1905 revolution. But Lenin and his party remembered the slogan 'All Power to the Soviets' and made it their own in the 1917 revolution. Similarly, no socialist organisation invented the flying picket, the working class did. But organised socialists remembered it and advocated them in every dispute that needs solidarity action to win.

A revolutionary organisation is part of the class, but doesn't dissolve itself into the class; tries to lead, but doesn't preach. It is the memory of the class, an educator and an organiser.

22. Democratic centralism

A revolutionary party of any serious size must be organised along democratic centralist lines. This phrase worries some people, or at least the word 'centralism' does. It seems to conjure the image of Stalinist parties with their bureaucratic, top-down style of leadership. Yet real democratic centralism has nothing to do with Stalinism. Rather, it is a method of organisation that, flows naturally from the position of the revolutionary organisation in the working class movement.

A revolutionary organisation strives to be the most advanced and resolute part of the working class movement. It is part of the class, but it is also politically separate from what many workers think a lot of the time and organisationally distinct from the reformist parties which reflect these ideas. There is therefore an unavoidable tension between a revolutionary organisation's desire to play as big a part as it can in the class struggle, to influence and recruit as many workers as possible, and the ideas of the workers who are not yet revolutionaries.

Democratic centralism is a way of ensuring that this tension between party and class is a creative tension, not a destructive tension.

If a party isn't democratic it cannot learn from the class struggle. Without its members being able to say what they have learnt in the course of the struggle, to argue what they think should be done next, to buttress their arguments with examples from the history of the movement, the organisation will remain a passive sect, not an interventionist network of organisers. Such a organisation may comment on the struggle but it will never lead it.

Without freedom of discussion the organisation can

never have effective unity. Members can only be convinced of a particular line of action on the basis of their own experience and on the basis of discussion and debate with other members. But unless, at the end of such discussion, a policy is decided which all members of the organisation carry out~unless there is centralism~there is no real democracy. A discussion which is followed by every member simply carrying on regardless of whether they are in the minority or the majority is not democratic. Indeed, it is not even organisation, since the whole purpose of organisation is to join together to pursue commonly agreed objectives.

There are organisations in the labour movement where debate and discussion is not followed by united action, the Labour Party being one of them. Labour Party conferences can decide what they like, and they can decide it as democratically as they like. But the Labour leadership simply ignores them. If the Labour leadership doesn't like a democratically decided policy it just doesn't get in the manifesto and it certainly doesn't get acted on in government.

The Labour Party is a bureaucratic centralist party. The democratic decisions of the membership are simply overridden by the dictates of the central bureaucracy.

The Labour Party behaves like this because its unacknowledged programme is to run capitalism, and if the struggle of the working class contradicts that aim, so much the worse for the working class. The aim of a revolutionary organisation on the other hand is to maximise the unity of the working class in the struggle against capitalism. To be able to do this all its members must be convinced of the party's politics and they must all act in a united way in trying to lead the struggles of the working class.

As Lenin said, 'The proletariat does not recognise unity in action without freedom to discuss and criticise'. That's why he described democratic centralism as 'freedom of discussion and criticism' followed by 'unity in action'.

How does a militant minority of activists in a revolutionary organisation influence others who are not revolutionaries?

The most important thing is that revolutionaries must be involved in the struggles of the day, be they demonstrations, strikes, rent boycotts, overtime bans, student occupations, anti war pickets or whatever. It is here, where people are already beginning to fight, that there is the best chance of changing things and of people developing socialist ideas. In such struggles socialists must aim to be the most active and inventive fighters. People will take revolutionary politics seriously if they see that it is of practical help in explaining and aiding their struggle.

So socialists must agitate and organise~suggest a way forward, point out the best methods of getting solidarity, build the confidence and involvement of all those affected by the issue in hand. This will often mean arguing with others~trade union bureaucrats, Labour councillors, the established leaders of tenants' associations or whatever.

If this is done in a fraternal and sensitive way people will listen. Even if you lose the argument you will group around you the people who most want to fight.

But as well as talking to people about the immediate struggle, revolutionaries should always raise more general issues. We should point out how this particular struggle fits into the wider battle against the government and the system. We should draw people's attention to international issues and to past struggles of the working class.

A website like Counterfire and the publications associated with it are invaluable in all this. It connects different struggles with one another. It connects individual struggles with the way the whole system runs. It reports the international struggles of the working class and the battle against imperialism. It tells the history of the workers' movement. It fights for anti racist and anti sexist ideas. Similarly, encouraging people to come to the meetings of a revolutionary organisation will help them to connect the struggle in which they are involved with wider socialist politics.

In doing all this there are two dangers which revolutionaries should avoid. The first is the danger of just going along with the ideas of the workers around you. This is easy to do. All the pressure from others in the social movements, Labour Party members and trade union officials, from workers who don't feel confident to fight or who don't see the connection between their bit of the class and other workers' will be in this direction. They will say: 'Don't be so militant', 'Slow things down a bit', 'Let's do things by the book'.

The pressures not to relate to the militant minority who want to fight, who can lead the majority if they argue with force and act with determination, are especially great in a country like Britain. Britain has a large and entrenched Labourite tradition which has every interest in bolstering the conservatism among workers, not in overcoming it. A different kind of inertia can even effect a revolutionary organisation. As Leon Trotsky wrote:

> *Each party, even the most revolutionary party, must inevitably produce its own organisational conservatism; for otherwise it would be lacking in the necessary stability. This is wholly a question of degree. In a revolutionary party the vitally necessary dose of conservatism must be combined with a complete freedom from routine, with initiative in orientation and daring in action. These qualities are put to the severest test during turning points in history.*

But in the battle against conservatism in the class, revolutionaries must be careful not to run too far ahead of the most militant workers. The point of organising the militant minority into an organisation is so they can lead the majority, not so they can rush off on their own and proclaim their revolutionary purity. Lenin made the point like this:

A vanguard performs its task as vanguard only when it is able to avoid being isolated from the mass of the people it leads and is able really to lead the whole mass forward.

This is why revolutionaries always seek common activity with other workers. We link arms on the picket line, even if the other strikers have racist or sexist ideas. And in the common struggle, especially if we succeed in stopping the scabs, we will stand every chance of convincing people that racism and sexism weaken the struggle and allow the bosses to divide us.

Not to link arms against a common enemy would be sectarian. Not to argue against racism or sexism would be an unprincipled retreat which will weaken both our organisation and the struggle.

Similarly, some workers who are willing to fight against the Tories may also still believe in immigration controls. To insist that they agree with us about immigration controls before we will join with them in fighting the Tories would be sectarian stupidity. The Tories will simply laugh as they defeat us one by one. Better to unite against the Tories and argue about why immigration controls are racist.

In this way we both maximise the working class' unity in action and build a principled revolutionary network which can ensure even greater success in future struggles.

Finally, revolutionaries should always urge others to join their organisation. People sometimes think that this is sectarian, that it amounts to putting the interests of our organisation before those of the working class. But this view misunderstands the relationship between revolutionary organisation and the class struggle. A stronger organisation means a stronger class. Consider, if fewer people had joined Counterfire from the anti-war movement there would not have been as many people to set up People's Assembly groups a few years later. And if fewer people had joined us from the People's Assemblies there would have been less people organised against the rise of UKIP.

Building a revolutionary party strengthens the struggle today and immeasurably strengthens the movement in the future.